Prevailing Prayer

WHAT HINDERS IT?

Prevailing Prayer

WHAT HINDERS IT?

BY

D. L. MOODY

AMBASSADOR

BELFAST ◆ GREENVILLE
NORTHERN IRELAND SOUTH CAROLINA

Prevailing Prayer
D. L. Moody

First Ambassador edition 1997
This edition 2001

ISBN 1 898787 93 X

Ambassador Publications
a division of
Ambassador Productions Ltd.,
Providence House
Ardenlee Street,
Belfast, BT6 8QJ
Northern Ireland
www.ambassador-productions.com

Emerald House Group Inc.
427 Wade Hampton Boulevard,
Greenville,
South Carolina 29609
United States of America
www.emeraldhouse.com

PREFATORY NOTE.

THE two first and essential means of grace are
the Word of God and Prayer. By these
comes Conversion ; for we are born again by
the Word of God which liveth and abideth
for ever ; and whosoever shall call upon the name of the
Lord shall be saved.

By these also we grow; for we are exhorted to
desire the sincere milk of the Word that we may grow
thereby ; and we cannot grow in grace and in the knowledge of the Lord Jesus Christ except we also speak to
Him in Prayer.

It is by the Word that the Father sanctifies us ; but
we are also bidden to watch and pray lest we enter into
temptation.

These two means of grace must be used in due proportion. If we read the Word and do not pray, we
may become puffed up with knowledge, without the

love that buildeth up. If we pray without reading the Word, we shall be ignorant of the mind and will of God, and become mystical and fanatical, and liable to be blown about by every wind of doctrine.

The following Addresses relate especially to Prayer ; but in order that our prayers may be for such things as are according to the will of God, they must be based upon the revelation of His own will to us : for of Him, and through Him, and to Him are all things ; and it is only by hearing His Word, in which we learn His purposes towards us and towards the world, that we can pray acceptably, praying in the Holy Ghost, asking those things which are pleasing in His sight.

These Addresses are not to be regarded as exhaustive, but suggestive. This great subject has been the theme of Prophets and Apostles, and of all good men in all ages of the world ; and my desire in sending forth this little volume is to encourage God's dear children to seek by prayer to move the Arm that moves the world.

D. L. Moody.

CONTENTS.

PRAYER was appointed to convey
  The blessings God designs to give ;
Long as they live should Christians pray,
  For only while they pray they live.

And shall we in dead silence lie,
  When Christ stands waiting for our prayer
My soul, thou hast a Friend on high ;
  Arise, and try thy interest there.

If pain afflict, or wrongs oppress ;
  If cares distract, or fears dismay ;
If guilt deject, if sin distress :
  The remedy's before thee—Pray !

Depend on Christ, thou canst not fail ;
  Make all thy wants and wishes known :
Fear not : His merits must prevail ;
  Ask what thou wilt : it shall be done !

                              Joseph Hart.

PREVAILING PRAYER.

CHAPTER I.

THE PRAYERS OF THE BIBLE.

THOSE who have left the deepest impression on this sin-cursed earth, have been men and women of prayer. You will find that PRAYER has been the mighty power that has moved not only God, but man. Abraham was a man of prayer; and angels came down from heaven to converse with him. Jacob's prayer was answered in the wonderful interview at Peniel, that resulted in his having such a mighty blessing, and in softening the heart of his brother Esau; the child Samuel was given in answer to Hannah's prayer; Elijah's prayer closed up the heavens for three years and six months; and he prayed again and the heavens gave rain.

The Apostle James tells us that the prophet Elijah was a man "subject to like passions as we are." I am thankful that those men and women who were so mighty in prayer were just like ourselves. We are apt to think that those prophets and mighty men and

women of old time were different from what we are. To
be sure they lived in a much darker age ; but they were
of like passions with ourselves.

We read that on another occasion Elijah brought
down fire on Mount Carmel. The prophets of Baal cried
long and loud ; but no answer came. The God of Elijah
heard and answered his prayer. Let us remember that the
God of Elijah still lives. The prophet was translated and
went up to heaven ; but his God still lives : and we have
the same access to Him that Elijah had.   We have the
same warrant to go to God and ask the fire from heaven
to come down and consume our lusts and passions—
to burn up our dross and let Christ shine through us.

Elisha prayed ; and life came back to a dead child.
Many of your children are dead in trespasses and sins.
Let us do as Elisha did ; let us entreat God to raise
them up in answer to our prayers.

Manasseh the king was a wicked man, and had
done everything he could against the God of his father ;
yet in Babylon, when he cried to God, his cry was
heard, and he was taken out of prison and put on the
throne at Jerusalem.   Surely if God gave heed to the
prayer of wicked Manasseh, He will hear ours in the
time of our distress.   Is not this a time of distress
with a great number of our fellow-men ?   Are there not
many among us whose hearts are burdened ?   As we go
to the throne of grace, let us remember that GOD
ANSWERS PRAYER.

Look, again, at Samson. He prayed ; and his strength
came back, so that he slew more at his death than during
his life.   He was a restored backslider, and he had power
with God. If those who have been backsliders will

but return to God, they will see how quickly God will answer prayer.

Job prayed; and his captivity was turned. Light came in the place of darkness, and God lifted him up above the height of his former prosperity—in answer to prayer.

Daniel prayed to God; and Gabriel came to tell him that he was a man greatly beloved of God. Three times that message came to him from heaven in answer to prayer. The secrets of heaven were imparted to him, and he was told that God's Son was going to be cut off for the sins of His people. We find also that Cornelius prayed; and Peter was sent to tell him words whereby he and his should be saved. In answer to prayer this great blessing came upon him and his household. Peter had gone up to the housetop to pray in the afternoon, when he had that wonderful vision of the sheet let down from heaven. It was when prayer was made without ceasing unto God for Peter, that the angel was sent to deliver him.

So all through the Scriptures you will find that when believing prayer went up to God, the answer came down. I think it would be a very interesting study to go right through the Bible and see what has happened while God's people have been on their knees calling upon Him. Perhaps the study would greatly strengthen our faith—showing, as it would, how wonderfully God has heard and delivered, when the cry has gone up to Him for help.

Look at Paul and Silas in the prison at Philippi. As they prayed and sang praises, the place was shaken; and the jailor was converted. Probably that one conversion has done more than any other recorded in the Bible to bring people into the Kingdom of God. How many have been blessed in seeking to answer the question—" What must I do to be saved?" It was the prayer of those two godly men that brought the jailor to his knees, and that brought blessing to him and his family.

You remember how Stephen, as he prayed and looked up, saw the heavens opened, and the Son of Man at the right hand of God: the light of heaven fell on his face so that it shone. Remember, too, how the face of Moses shone as he came down from the Mount: he had been in communion with God. So when we get really into communion with God, He lifts up His countenance upon us; and instead of our having gloomy looks, our faces will shine, because God has heard and answered our prayers.

I want to call your special attention to Christ as an example for us in this matter of prayer. He was an example for us in all things; in nothing more than in prayer. We read that Christ prayed to His Father for everything. Every great crisis in His life was preceded by prayer. Let me quote a few passages. I never noticed till a few years ago that Christ was praying at His baptism. As He prayed, the heaven was opened, and the Holy Ghost descended on Him. Another great event in His life was His Transfiguration. "As He prayed, the fashion of His countenance was altered, and His raiment was white and glistering."

We read again: " It came to pass in those days that He went out into a mountain to pray, and continued all night in prayer to God." This is the only place where it is recorded that the Saviour spent a whole night in prayer. What was about to take place? When He came down from the mountain He gathered His disciples around Him, and preached that great discourse known as the Sermon on the Mount—the most wonderful sermon that has ever been preached to mortal men. Probably no sermon has done so much good; and it was preceded by a night of prayer. If our sermons are going to reach the hearts and consciences of the people, we must be much in prayer to God, that there may be power with the word.

In the Gospel of John we read that Jesus at the grave of Lazarus lifted up His eyes to Heaven, and said, "Father, I thank Thee that Thou hast heard Me: and I know that Thou hearest Me always; but because of the people which stand by I said it, that they may believe that Thou hast sent Me." Notice, that before He spoke the dead to life He spoke to His Father. If our spiritually dead ones are to be raised, we must first get power with God. The reason we so often fail in moving our fellow-men is that we try to win them without first getting power with God. Jesus was in communion with His Father; and so He could be assured that His prayers were heard.

We read again, in the twelfth of John, that He prayed to the Father. I think this is one of the saddest chapters in the whole Bible. He was about to leave the Jewish nation and to make atonement for the sin of the world. Hear what He says: "Now is My soul troubled; and what shall I say? Father, save Me from this hour: but for this cause came I unto this hour." He was almost under the shadow of the Cross; the iniquities of mankind were about to be laid upon Him ; one of His twelve disciples was going to deny Him, and swear he never knew Him ; another was to sell Him for thirty pieces of silver; all were to forsake Him and flee. His soul was exceeding sorrowful, and He prays ; when His soul was troubled, God spake to Him. Then in the Garden of Gethsemane, while He prayed, an angel appeared to strengthen Him. In answer to His cry, " Father, glorify Thy name," He hears a voice coming down from the glory—" I have both glorified it, and will glorify it again."

Another memorable prayer of our Lord was in the Garden of Gethsemane : " He was withdrawn from them about a stone's cast, and kneeled down, and prayed." I would draw your attention to the recorded fact that four times the answer came right down from heaven while the Saviour prayed to God. The first time was at His baptism, when the heavens were opened and the Spirit descended upon Him in answer to His prayer. Again, on the Mount of Transfiguration, God appeared and spoke to Him. Then when the Greeks came desiring to see Him, the voice of God was heard responding to His call; and again when He cried to the Father in the midst of His agony, a direct response was given. These things are recorded, I doubt not, that we may be encouraged to pray.

We read that His disciples came to Him, and said, " Lord, teach us to pray." It is not recorded that He taught them how to preach. I have often said that I would rather know how to pray like Daniel than to preach like Gabriel. If you get love into your soul, so that the grace of God may come down in answer to prayer, there will be no trouble about reaching the people. It is not by eloquent sermons that perishing souls are going to be reached ; we need the power of God in order that the blessing may come down.

The prayer our Lord taught His disciples is commonly called the Lord's Prayer. I think that the Lord's prayer, more properly, is that in the seventeenth of John. That is the longest prayer on record that Jesus made. You can read it slowly and carefully in about four or five minutes. I think we may learn a lesson here. Our Master's prayers were short when offered in public ; when He was alone with God that was a different thing, and He could spend the whole night in communion with His Father. My experience is that those who pray most in their closets generally make short prayers in public. Long prayers are too often not prayers at all ; and they weary the people. How short the publican's prayer was : " God be merciful to me a sinner ! " The Syrophenician woman's was shorter still : " Lord, help me ! " She went right to the mark, and she got what she wanted. The prayer of the thief on the cross was a short one : " Lord, remember me when Thou comest into Thy Kingdom ! " Peter's prayer was, " Lord, save me : or I perish ! " So, if you go through the Scriptures, you will find that the prayers that brought immediate answers were generally brief. Let our prayers be to the point, just telling God what we want.

In the prayer of our Lord, in John seventeen, we find that He made seven requests—one for Himself, four for His disciples around Him, and two for the disciples of succeeding ages. Six times in that one prayer He repeats that God had sent Him. The world looked upon Him as an impostor ; and He wanted them to know that He was Heaven-sent. He speaks of the world nine times, and makes mention of His disciples and those who believe on Him, fifty times.

Christ's last prayer on the Cross was a short one : " Father, forgive them : for they know not what they do." I believe that prayer was answered. We find that right there, in front of the Cross, a Roman centurion was converted. It was probably in answer to the Saviour's prayer. The conversion of the thief, I believe, was in answer to that prayer of our blessed Lord. Saul of Tarsus may have heard it ; and the words may have followed him as he travelled to Damascus : so that when the Lord spoke to him on the way, he may have recognized the voice. One thing we do know : that on the Day of Pentecost some of the enemies of the Lord were converted. Surely that was in answer to the prayer : " Father, forgive them ! "

Hence we see that prayer holds a high place among the exercises of a spiritual life. All God's people have been praying people. Look, for instance, at Baxter ! He stained his study walls with praying breath ; and after he was anointed with the unction of the Holy Ghost, sent a river of living water over Kidderminster, and converted hundreds. Luther and his coadjutors were men of such mighty pleading with God, that they broke the spell of ages, and laid nations subdued at the foot of the Cross. John Knox grasped all Scotland in his strong arms of faith : his prayers terrified tyrants.

Whitefield, after much holy, faithful closet-pleading, went to the Devil's fair ; and took more than a thousand souls out of the paw of the lion in one day. See a praying Wesley turn more than ten thousand souls to the Lord ! Look at the praying Finney, whose prayers, faith, sermons, and writings, have shaken the half of America, and sent a wave of blessing through the British churches !

Dr. Guthrie thus speaks of prayer and its necessity : " The first true sign of spiritual life, prayer, is also the means of maintaining it. Man can as well live physically without breathing, as spiritually without praying. There is a class of animals—the cetaceous, neither fish nor sea-fowl, that inhabit the deep. It is their home ; they never leave it for the shore ; yet, though swimming beneath its waves, and sounding its darkest depths, they have ever and anon to rise to the surface that they may breathe the air. Without that, these monarchs of the deep could not exist in the dense element in which they live, and move, and have their being. And some-thing like what is imposed on them by a physical neces-sity, the Christian has to do by a spiritual one. It is by ever and anon ascending up to God, by rising through prayer into a loftier, purer region for supplies of Divine grace, that he maintains his spiritual life. Prevent these animals from rising to the surface, and they die for want of breath ; prevent the Christian from rising to God, and he dies for want of prayer. 'Give me children,' cried Rachel, 'or else I die.' 'Let me breathe,' says a man gasping, 'or else I die.' 'Let me pray,' says the Chris-tian, 'or else I die.' "

"Since I began," said Dr. Payson when a student, "to beg God's blessing on my studies, I have done more in one week than in the whole year before." Luther, when most pressed with work, said, " I have so much to do that I cannot get on without three hours a day praying." And not only do theologians think and speak highly of prayer; men of all ranks and positions in life have felt the same. General Havelock rose at four o'clock, if the hour for marching was six, rather than lose the precious privilege of communion with God before setting out. Sir Matthew Hale says, "If I omit praying and reading God's Word in the morning, nothing goes well all day."

"A great part of my time," said McCheyne, "is spent in getting my heart in tune for prayer. It is the link that connects earth with Heaven."

A comprehensive view of the subject will show that there are nine elements which are essential to true prayer. The first is Adoration ; we cannot meet God on a level at the start. We must approach Him as One far beyond our reach or ken. The next is Confession ; sin must be put out of the way. We cannot have any communion with God while there is any transgression between us. If there stands some wrong you have done a man, you cannot expect that man's favour until you go to him and confess the fault. Restitution is another ; we have to make good the wrong, wherever possible. Thanksgiving is the next ; we must be thankful for what God has done for us already. Then comes Forgiveness ; and then Unity ; and then for prayer, such as these things produce, there must be Faith. Thus influenced, we shall be ready to offer direct Petition. We hear a good deal of praying that is just exhorting ; and if you did not see the man's eyes closed, you would suppose he was preaching. Then, much that is called prayer is simply finding fault. There needs to be more *petition* in our prayers. After all these, there must come Submission. While praying, we must be ready to accept the will of God. We shall proceed to consider these nine elements in detail, closing our inquiries by giving incidents illustrative of the certainty of our receiving, under such conditions, Answers to Prayer.

" Lord, what a change within us one short hour
 Spent in Thy presence will prevail to make !
 What heavy burdens from our bosoms take :
What parchèd grounds refresh as with a shower.

" We kneel—and all around us seems to lower :
 We rise—and all, the distant and the near,
 Stands forth in sunny outline brave and clear ;
We kneel : how weak !—we rise : how full of power !

" Why, therefore, should we do ourselves this wrong,
 Or others—that we are not always strong ?—
That we are ever overborne with care ;—
 That we should ever weak or heartless be,
Anxious or troubled, while with us is prayer,
 And joy, and strength, and courage, are with Thee ? "

Trench.

CHAPTER II.

ADORATION.

THIS has been defined as the act of rendering Divine honour, including in it reverence, esteem, and love. It literally signifies to apply the hand to the mouth, " to kiss the hand "; in Eastern countries this is one of the great marks of respect and submission. The importance of coming before God in this spirit is great ; hence it is often impressed upon us in the Word of God.

The Rev. Newman Hall, in his work on the Lord's Prayer, says : " Man's worship, apart from revelation, has been uniformly characterized by selfishness. We come to God either to thank Him for benefits already received, or to implore still further benefits : food, raiment, health, safety, comfort. Like Jacob at Bethel, we are disposed to make the worship we render to God correlative with 'food to eat, and raiment to put on.' This style of petition, in which self generally precedes and predominates, if it does not altogether absorb, our supplications, is not only seen in the votaries of false systems, but in the majority of the prayers of professed Cirhstians. Our prayers are like the Parthian horsemen, who ride one way while they look another; we seem to go toward God; but, indeed, reflect upon ourselves. And this may be the reason why many times our prayers are sent forth, like the raven out of Noah's ark, and never return. But when we make the glory of God the chief end of our devotion, they go forth like the dove, and return to us again with an olive branch."

Let me refer you to a passage in the prophecies of Daniel. He was one of the men who knew how to pray; his prayer brought the blessing of Heaven upon himself and upon his people. He says: "I set my face unto the Lord God, to seek by prayer and supplications, with fasting, and sackcloth, and ashes: and I prayed unto the Lord my God, and made my confession; and said, O Lord, the great and dreadful God, keeping the covenant and mercy to them that love Him, and to them that keep His commandments!"

The thought I want to call your special attention to is conveyed in the words, "O Lord, the grate and dreadful God!" Daniel took his right place before God—in the dust; he put God in His right place. It was when Abraham was on his face, prostrate before God, that God spoke to him. Holiness belongs to God; sinfulness belongs to us.

Brooks, that grand old Puritan writer, says, "A person of real holiness is much affected and taken up in the admiration of the holiness of God. Unholy persons may be somewhat affected and taken with the other excellences of God; it is only holy souls that are taken and affected with His holiness. The more holy any are, the more deeply are they affected by this. To the holy angels, the holiness of God is the sparkling diamond in the ring of glory. But unholy persons are affected

and taken with anything rather than with this. Nothing
strikes the sinner into such a damp as a discourse on the
holiness of God ; it is as the handwriting on the wall ;
nothing makes the head and heart of a sinner to ache
like a sermon upon the Holy One ; nothing galls and
gripes, nothing stings and terrifies unsanctified ones, like
a lively setting forth of the holiness of God. But to
holy souls there are no discourses that do more suit and
satisfy them, that do more delight and content them,
that do more please and profit them, than those that do
most fully and powerfully discover God to be glorious
in holiness." So, in coming before God, we must adore
and reverence His name.

The same thing is brought out in Isaiah :

"In the year that king Uzziah died, I saw also the
Lord sitting upon a throne, high and lifted up ; and His
train filled the temple. Above it stood the seraphim ;
each one had six wings : with twain he covered his
face, and with twain he covered his feet, and with twain
he did fly. And one cried unto another, and said : Holy,
holy, holy, is the Lord of hosts : the whole earth is full
of His glory."

When we see the holiness of God, we shall adore and
magnify Him. Moses had to learn the same lesson.
God told him to take his shoes from off his feet, for the
place whereon he stood was holy ground. When we hear
men trying to make out that they are holy, and speaking about their holiness, they make light of the holiness
of God. It is His holiness that we need to think and
speak about : when we do that, we shall be prostrate in
the dust. You remember, also, how it was with Peter.
When Christ made Himself known to him, he said,

" Depart from me, for I am a sinful man, O Lord!" A sight of God is enough to show us how holy He is, and how unholy we are.

We find that Job too, had to be taught the same lesson. " Then Job answered the Lord, and said: Behold I am vile: what shall I answer Thee? I will lay my hand upon my mouth."

As you hear Job discussing with his friends you would think he was one of the holiest men that ever lived. He was eyes to the blind, and feet to the lame; he fed the hungry, and clothed the naked. What a wonderfully good man he was! It was all I, I, I. At last God said to him, " Gird up your loins like a man; and I will put a few questions to you." The moment that God revealed Himself, Job changed his language. He saw his own vileness, and God's purity. He said, " I have heard of Thee by the hearing of the ear; but now mine eye seeth Thee: wherefore I abhor myself, and repent in dust and ashes."

The same thing is seen in the cases of those who came to our Lord in the days of His flesh; those who came aright, seeking and obtaining the blessing, manifested a lively sense of His infinite superiority to themselves. The Centurion, of whom we read in the eighth of Matthew, said, " Lord, I am not worthy that Thou shouldest come under my roof;" Jairus "worshipped Him," as he presented his request; the leper, in the Gospel of Mark, came "kneeling down to Him;" the Syrophenician woman "came and fell at His feet;" the man full of leprosy "seeing Jesus, fell on his face." So too the beloved disciple, speaking of the feeling they had concerning Him when they were abiding with Him as their Lord, said : " We beheld His glory, the glory as of the only-begotten of the Father, full of grace and truth ; " however intimate their companionship, and tender their love, they reverenced as much as they communed, and adored as much as they loved.

We may say of every act of prayer as George Herbert says of public worship :

" When once thy foot enters the Church, be bare ;
God is more there than thou : for thou art there
Only by His permission. Then beware.
And make thyself all reverence and fear.
Kneeling ne'er spoiled silk stocking ; quit thy state :
All equal are within the Church's gate."

The wise man says, " Keep thy foot when thou goest to the house of God ; and be more ready to hear than to give the sacrifice of fools : for they consider not that they do evil. Be not rash with thy mouth ; and let not thine heart be hasty to utter anything before God : for God is in heaven, and thou upon earth—therefore let thy words be few."

If we are struggling to live a higher life, and to know something of God's holiness and purity, what we need is to be brought into contact with Him, that He may reveal Himself. Then we shall take our place before Him as those men of old were constrained to do. We shall hallow His Name—as the Master taught His disciples, when He said, " Hallowed be Thy Name ! " When I think of the irreverence of the present time, it seems to me that we have fallen on evil days.

Let us, as Christians, when we draw near to God in prayer, give Him His right place. " Let us have grace whereby we may serve God acceptably, with reverence and godly fear, for our God is a consuming fire."

"Thou dear and great mysterious **Three,**
  For ever be adored
For all the endless grace we see
  In our Redeemer stored !

" The Father's ancient grace we sing,
  That chose us in our Head ;
Ordaining Christ, our God and **King,**
  To suffer in our stead.

" The sacred Son, in equal strains,
  With reverence we address,
For all His grace, and dying pains,
  And splendid righteousness.

" With tuneful tongue the Holy Ghost
  For His great work we praise,
Whose power inspires the blood-bought host
  Their grateful voice to raise.

" Thus the Eternal Three in One
  We join to praise, for grace
And endless glory through the Son,
  As shining from His face."

CHAPTER III.

CONFESSION.

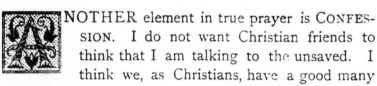NOTHER element in true prayer is CONFES-
SION. I do not want Christian friends to
think that I am talking to the unsaved. I
think we, as Christians, have a good many
sins to confess.

If you go back to the Scripture records, you will
find that the men who lived nearest to God, and had
most power with Him, were those who confessed their
sins and failures. Daniel, as we have seen, confessed his
sins and those of his people. Yet there is nothing recorded against Daniel. He was one of the best men then
on the face of the earth; yet was his confession of sin
one of the deepest and most humble on record. Brooks,
referring to Daniel's Confession, says: "In these words
you have seven circumstances that Daniel useth in confessing of his and the people's sins: and all to heighten
and aggravate them. First, 'We have sinned'; secondly,
'We have committed iniquity'; thirdly, 'We have done
wickedly'; fourthly, 'We have rebelled against Thee';
fifthly, 'We have departed from Thy precepts'; sixthly,
'We have not hearkened unto Thy servants'; seventhly,

'Nor our princes, nor all the people of the land.' These seven aggravations which Daniel reckons up in his confession are worthy our most serious considera- tion."

Job was no doubt a holy man, a mighty prince; yet he had to fall in the dust and confess his sins. So you will find it all through the Scriptures. When Isaiah saw the purity and holiness of God, he beheld himself in his true light; and he exclaimed, "Woe is me! for I am undone; because I am a man of unclean lips."

I firmly believe that the Church of God will have to confess their own sins, before there can be any great work of grace in London, or in any other place. There must be a deeper work among God's believing people. I sometimes think it is about time to give up preach- ing to the ungodly, and preach to those who pro- fess to be Christians. If we had a higher standard of life in the Church of God, there would be thousands more flocking into the Kingdom. So it was in the past; when God's believing children turned away from their sins and their idols, then the fear of God fell upon the people round about. Take up the history of Israel, and you find that when they put away their strange gods, God visited the nation, and there came a mighty work of grace.

What we want in these days is a true and deep revival in the Church of God. I have little sympathy with the idea that God is going to reach the outlying masses by a cold and formal Church. The judgment of God must begin with us. You notice that when Daniel got that wonderful answer to prayer recorded in the ninth chapter, ne was confessing his sin. That is one of the best chapters on prayer in the whole Bible. We read :

" Whiles I was speaking, and praying, and confessing my sin, and the sin of my people Israel, and presenting my supplication before the Lord my God for the holy mountain of my God ; yea, whiles I was speaking in my prayer, even the man Gabriel, whom I had seen in the vision at the beginning, being caused to fly swiftly, touched me about the time of the evening oblation. And he informed me, and talked with me, and said, O Daniel, I am now come forth to give thee skill and understanding."

So, also, when Job was confessing his sin, God turned his captivity and heard his prayer. God will hear our prayer and turn our captivity when we take our true place before Him, and confess and forsake our transgressions. It was when Isaiah cried out before the Lord, " I am undone," that the blessing came ; the live coal was taken from the altar and put upon his lips ; and he went out to write one of the most wonderful books the world has ever seen. What a blessing it has been to the Church !

It was when David said, " I have sinned !" that God dealt in mercy with him. " I acknowledged my sin unto Thee, and mine iniquity have I not hid. I said, I will confess my transgressions unto the Lord ; and Thou forgavest the iniquity of my sin." Notice how David made a very similar confession to that of the prodigal in the fifteenth of Luke : " I acknowledge my transgressions ; and my sin is ever before me. Against Thee, Thee only, have I sinned, and done this evil in Thy sight !" There is no difference between the king and the beggar when the Spirit of God comes into the heart and convicts of sin.

Richard Sibbes quaintly says of Confession : " This is the way to give glory to God : when we have laid open our souls to God, and laid as much against ourselves as the devil could do that way. For, let us think what the devil would lay to our charge at the hour of death and the day of judgment. He would lay hard to our charge this and that—let us accuse ourselves as he would, and as he will ere long. The more we accuse and judge ourselves, and set up a tribunal in our hearts, certainly there will follow an incredible ease. Jonah was cast into the sea, and there was ease in the ship ; Achan was stoned, and the plague was stayed. Out with Jonah, out with Achan ; and there will follow ease and quiet in the soul presently. Conscience will receive wonderful ease.

" It must needs be so ; for when God is honoured, conscience is purified. God is honoured by confession of sin every way. It honours His omniscience, that He is all-seeing ; that He sees our sins and searches our hearts —our secrets are not hid from Him. It honours His power. What makes us confess our sins, but that we are afraid of His power, lest He should execute it ? and what makes us confess our sins, but that we know there is mercy with Him that He may be feared, and that there is pardon for sin ? We would not confess our sins else. With men it is, Confess, and have execution ; but with God, Confess, and have mercy. It is His own protesta-tion. We should never lay open our sins but for mercy. So it honours God : and when He is honoured, He honours the soul with inward peace and tranquillity."

Old Thomas Fuller says : " Man's owning his weakness is the only stock for God thereon to graft the grace of His assistance."

Confession implies humility ; and this, in God's sight, is of great price.

A farmer went with his son into a wheat field, to see if it was ready for the harvest. " See, father," exclaimed the boy, " how straight these stems hold up their heads ! They must be the best ones. Those that hang their heads down, I am sure, cannot be good for much." The farmer plucked a stalk of each kind and said, " See here, foolish child ! This stalk that stood so straight is light-headed, and almost good for nothing ; while this that. hung its head so modestly is full of the most beautiful grain."

Outspokenness is needful and powerful, both with God and man. We need to be honest and frank with ourselves. A soldier said in a revival meeting, " My fellow-soldiers, I am not excited ; I am *convinced*—that is all. I feel that I ought to be a Christian ; that I ought to say so, to tell you so, and to ask you to come with me : and now, if there is a call for sinners seeking Christ to come forward, I for one shall go—not to make a show, for I have nothing but sin to show. I do not go because I want to—I would rather keep my seat ; but going will be telling the truth. I ought to be a Christian, I want to be a Christian ; and going forward for prayers is just telling the truth about it." More than a score went with him.

Speaking of Pharaoh's words, " Entreat the Lord that He may take away the frogs from me," Mr. Spurgeon says, " A fatal flaw is manifest in that prayer. *It contains no confession of sin.* He says not, ' I have rebelled against the Lord ; entreat that I may find for-giveness !' Nothing of the kind ; he loves sin as much as ever. A prayer without penitence is a prayer without acceptance. If no tear has fallen upon it, it is withered. Thou must come to God as a sinner through a Saviour, but by no other way. He that comes to God like the Pharisee, with, ' God, I thank Thee that I am not as other men are,' never draws near to God at all ; but he that cries, ' God be merciful to me a sinner,' has come to God by the way which God has Himself appointed. There must be confession of sin before God, or our prayer is faulty."

If this confession of sin is deep among believers, it will be so among the ungodly also. I never knew it to fail. I am so anxious that God should revive His work in our own hearts, so that we may see the exceeding sinfulness of sin. There are a great many fathers and mothers among us who are anxious for the conversion of their children. I suppose I have had not less than fifty messages from parents come to me within the past ten days, wondering why their children are not saved. I venture to say that, as a rule, the fault lies at our own door. There may be something in our life that stands in the way. It may be there is some secret sin that keeps back the blessing. David lived in the awful sin into which he fell, for many months before Nathan made his appearance. Let us pray God to come into our hearts to-day, and make His power felt. If it is a right eye, let us pluck it out ; if it is a right hand, let us cut it off ; that we may have power with God and with man.

Why is it that so many of our children are wandering off into the public-house, and drifting away into infidelity

—going down to a dishonoured grave? There seems to be very little power in the Christianity of the present time. Many godly parents find that their children are going astray. Does it arise from some secret sin clinging around the heart? There is a passage of God's Word that is often quoted; but in ninety-nine cases out of a hundred those who quote it stop at the wrong place. In the fifty-ninth of Isaiah we read : " Behold, the Lord's hand is not shortened, that it cannot save; neither His ear heavy, that it cannot hear." There they stop. Of course God's hand is not shortened, and his ear is not heavy; but we ought to read the next verse : " Your iniquities have separated between you and your God; and your sins have hid His face from you, that He will not hear. For your hands are defiled with blood, and your fingers with iniquity; your lips have spoken lies, your tongue hath muttered perverseness." As Matthew Henry says, " It was owing to themselves—they stood in their own light ; they shut their own door. God was coming towards them in the way of mercy, and they hindered Him. '*Your iniquities have kept good things from you.*' "

Bear in mind that if we are regarding iniquity in our hearts, or living on a mere empty profession, we have no claim to expect that our prayers will be answered. There is not one solitary promise for us. I sometimes tremble when I hear people get up and quote promises, and say that God is bound to fulfil those promises to them ; when all the time there is something in their own life which they are not willing to give up. It is well for us to search our hearts, and find out why it is that our prayers are not answered.

That is a very solemn passage in Isaiah :—

" Hear the word of the Lord, ye rulers of Sodom ; give ear unto the law of our God, ye people of Gomorrah. To what purpose is the multitude of your sacrifices unto me ? saith the Lord : I am full of the burnt-offerings of rams, and the fat of fed beasts ; and I delight not in the blood of bullocks, or of lambs, or of he goats. When ye come to appear before Me, who hath required this at your hand, to tread My courts ? Bring no more vain oblations : incense is an abomination unto Me ; the new moons and sabbaths, the calling of assemblies, I cannot away with—it is iniquity, even the solemn meeting."

" Even the solemn meeting ! "—think of that. If God does not get our heart-service, He will have none of it ; it is an abomination to Him.

" Your new moons and your appointed feasts My soul hateth : they are a trouble unto Me ; I am weary to bear them. And when ye spread forth your hands, I will hide Mine eyes from you : yea, when ye make many prayers, I will not hear : your hands are full of blood. Wash you, make you clean ; put away the evil of your doings from before Mine eyes ; cease to do evil ; learn to do well ; seek judgment, relieve the oppressed, judge the fatherless, plead for the widow. Come now, and let us reason together, saith the Lord ; though your sins be as scarlet, they shall be as white as snow ; though they be red like crimson, they shall be as wool."

Again we read in Proverbs : " He that turneth away his ear from hearing the law, even his prayer shall be abomination." Think of that ! It may shock some of us to think that our prayers are an abomination to God ; yet if any are living in known sin, this is what God's Word says about them. If we are not willing to

turn from sin and obey God's law, we have no right to
expect that He will answer our prayers. Unconfessed
sin is unforgiven sin ; and unforgiven sin is the darkest,
foulest thing on this sin-cursed earth. You cannot find
a case in the Bible where a man has been honest in dealing with sin, but God has been honest with him and
blessed him. The prayer of the humble and the contrite
heart is a delight to God. There is no sound that goes
up from this sin-cursed earth so sweet to His ear as the
prayer of the man who is walking uprightly.

Let me call your attention to that prayer of David
in which he says : " Search me, O God, and know my
heart ; try me, and know my thoughts ; and see if there
be any wicked way in me, and lead me in the way ever-
lasting !" I wish all my readers would commit these
verses to memory. If we should all honestly make this
prayer once every day there would be a good deal of
change in our lives. " *Search* ME "—not my neighbour.
It is so easy to pray for other people, but so hard to get
home to ourselves. I am afraid that we who are busy in
the Lord's work, are very often in danger of neglecting
our own vineyard. In this Psalm, David got home to
himself. There is a difference between God searching
me and my searching myself. I may search my heart,
and pronounce it all right ; but when God searches me
as with a lighted candle, a good many things will come
to light that perhaps I knew nothing about.

" *Try me.*" David was tried when he fell by taking
his eye off from the God of his father Abraham. " *Know
my thoughts.*" God looks at the thoughts. Are our
thoughts pure ? Have we in our hearts thoughts against
God or against His people—against any one in the

world? If we have, we are not right in the sight of God.
Oh, may God search us, every one! I do not know any
better prayer that we can make than this prayer of
David. One of the most solemn things in the Scripture
history is that when holy men—better men than we are
—were tested and tried, they were found to be as weak
as water away from God.

Now, dear friends, let us be sure that we are right.
Isaac Ambrose, in his work on " Self Trial," has the
following pithy words : " Now and then propose we
to our hearts these two questions : 1. ' Heart, how dost
thou ? ' "—a few words, but a very serious question.
You know this is the first question and the first salute
that we use to one another—How do you do ? I
would to God we sometimes thus spoke to our hearts :
Heart, how dost thou ? how is it with thee, for thy
spiritual state ? " 2. ' Heart, what wilt thou do ? ' or,
' Heart, what dost thou think will become of thee and
me ? '—as that dying Roman once said : ' Poor wretched
miserable soul, whither art thou and I going ?—and what
will become of thee, when thou and I shall part ? '

" This very thing does Moses propose to Israel, though
in other terms, ' Oh that they would consider their latter
end ! '—and oh that we would propose this question constantly to our hearts, to consider and debate upon! 'Commune with your own hearts,' said David ; that is, debate
the matter betwixt you and your own hearts to the very
utmost. Let your hearts be so put to it in communing
with them, as that they may speak their very bottom.
Commune—or hold a serious communication, and clear
intelligence and acquaintance—with your own hearts."

It was the confession of a divine, sensible of his

neglect, and especially of the difficulty of this duty : " I
have lived," said he, " forty years and somewhat more, and
carried my heart in my bosom all this while ; and yet my
heart and I are as great strangers, and as utterly unacquainted, as if we had never come near one another.
Nay, I know not my heart ; I have forgotten my heart.
Alas ! alas ! that I could be grieved at the very heart,
that my poor heart and I have been so unacquainted !
We are fallen into an Athenian age, spending our time
in nothing more than in telling or hearing news. How
go things here ? How there ? How in one place ? How
in another ?   But who is there that is inquisitive—How
are things with my poor heart ? Weigh but in the
balance of a serious consideration, what time we have
spent in this duty, and what time otherwise : and for
many scores and hundreds of hours or days that we owe
to our hearts in this duty, can we write fifty ? or where
there should have been fifty vessels full of this duty, can
we find twenty, or ten ? Oh, the days, months, years, we
bestow upon sin, vanity, the affairs of this world ! whiles
we afford not a minute in converse with our own hearts
concerning their case."

If there is anything in our lives that is wrong, let us
ask God to show it to us. Have we been selfish ? Have
we been more jealous of our own reputation than of the
honour of God ?   Elijah thought he was very jealous for
the honour of God ; but it turned out that it was his own
honour after all—self was really at the bottom of it.
One of the saddest things, I think, that Christ had to
meet with in His disciples was this very thing ; there
was a constant struggle between them as to who
should be the greatest, instead of each one taking

the humblest place and being least in his own estimation.

We are told in proof of this, that "He came to Capernaum: and being in the house He asked them, What was it that ye disputed among yourselves by the way? But they held their peace; for by the way they had disputed among themselves, who should be the greatest. And He sat down, and called the twelve, and saith unto them, If any man desire to be first, the same shall be last of all, and servant of all. And He took a child, and set him in the midst of them; and when He had taken him in His arms, He said unto them, Whosoever shall receive one of such children in My name, receiveth Me: and whosoever shall receive Me, receiveth not Me, but Him that sent Me."

Soon after, "James and John, the sons of Zebedee, come unto Him, saying, Master, we would that Thou shouldest do for us whatsoever we shall desire. And He said unto them, What would ye that I should do for you? They said unto Him, Grant unto us that we may sit, one on Thy right hand, and the other on Thy left hand, in Thy glory. But Jesus said unto them, Ye know not what ye ask: can ye drink of the cup that I drink of?—and be baptized with the baptism that I am baptized with? And they said unto Him, We can. And Jesus said unto them, Ye shall indeed drink of the cup that I drink of; and with the baptism that I am baptized withal shall ye be baptized: but to sit on My right hand and on My left hand is not Mine to give; but it shall be given to them for whom it is prepared. And when the ten heard it, they began to be much displeased with James and John. But Jesus called them to

Him, and saith unto them, Ye know that they which are accounted to rule over the Gentiles exercise lordship over them ; and their great ones exercise authority upon them.   But so shall it not be among you : but whosoever will be great among you, shall be your minister ; and whosoever of you will be the chiefest, shall be servant of all.   For even the Son of Man came not to be ministered unto, but to minister, and to give His life a ransom for many."

The latter words were spoken in the third year of His ministry.   Three years the disciples had been with Him : they had listened to the words that fell from His lips ; yet they had failed to learn this lesson of humility.   The most humiliating thing that happened among the chosen twelve occurred on the night of our Lord's betrayal, when Judas sold Him, and Peter denied Him.   If there was any place where there should have been an absence of these thoughts, it was at the Supper-table.   Yet we find that when Christ instituted that blessed memorial there was a debate going on among His disciples who should be the greatest.   Think of that !—right under the Cross, when the Master was " exceeding sorrowful, even unto death," was already tasting the bitterness of Calvary, and the horrors of that dark hour were gathering upon His soul.

I think if God searches us, we will find a good many things in our lives for us to confess.   If we are tried and tested by God's law, there will be many, many things that will have to be changed.   I ask again, Are we selfish or jealous ?   Are we willing to hear of others being used by God more than we are ?   Are our Church of England friends willing to hear of a great revival of

God's work among Dissenters? Would it rejoice their soul to hear of such efforts being blessed? Are Dissenters willing to hear of a reviving of God's work in the Church of England? If we are full of narrow, party, and sectarian feelings, there will be many things to be laid aside. Let us pray to God to search us, and try us, and see if there be any evil way in us. If these holy and good men felt that they were faulty, should we not tremble, and endeavour to find out if there is anything in our lives that God would have us get rid of?

Once again, let me call your attention to the **prayer** of David contained in the fifty-first Psalm. A friend of mine told me some years ago that he repeated this prayer as his own every week. I think it would be a good thing if we offered up these petitions frequently; let them go right up from our hearts. If we have been proud, or irritable, or lacking in patience, shall we not at once confess it? Is it not time that we began at home, and got our lives straightened out? See how quickly the ungodly will then begin to inquire the way of life! Let those of us who are parents set our own houses in order, and be filled with Christ's Spirit; then it will not be long before our children will be inquiring what they must do to get the same Spirit. I believe that to-day, by its lukewarmness and formality, the Christian Church is making more infidels than all the books that infidels ever wrote. I do not fear infidel lectures half so much as the cold and dead formalism in the professing Church at the present time. One prayer-meeting, like that the disciples had on the day of Pentecost, would shake the whole infidel fraternity.

What we want is to get hold of God in prayer. You

are not going to reach the masses by great sermons. We want to move the Arm that moves the world. To do that, we must be clear and right before God. "For if our heart condemn us, God is greater than our heart, and knoweth all things. Beloved, if our heart condemn us not, then have we confidence toward God; and whatsoever we ask, we receive of Him, because we keep His commandments, and do those things that are pleasing in His sight."

" No, not despairingly
    Come I to Thee ;
No, not distrustingly
    Bend I the knee ;
Sin hath gone over me,
Yet is this still my plea,
    Jesus hath died.

" Ah, mine iniquity
    Crimson has been ;
Infinite, infinite,
    Sin upon sin ;
Sin of not loving Thee,
Sin of not trusting Thee
    Infinite sin.

" Lord, I confess to Thee
    Sadly my sin ;
All I am, tell I Thee,
    All I have been.
Purge Thou my sin away,
Wash Thou my soul this day :
    Lord, make me clean ! "—*Dr. H. Bonar.*

CHAPTER IV.

RESTITUTION.

THIRD element of successful prayer is RESTI-
TUTION.   If I have at any time taken what
does not belong to me, and am not willing
to make restitution, my prayers will not go
very far towards heaven.   It is a singular thing, but I
have never touched on this subject in my addresses,
without hearing of immediate results.   A man once
told me that I would not need to dwell on this point at
a meeting I was about to address, as probably there
would be no one present that would need to make restitution.   But I think if the Spirit of God searches our
hearts, we shall most of us find a good many things
have to be done that we never thought of before.

After Zaccheus met with Christ, things looked altogether different.   I venture to say that the idea of making restitution never entered into his mind before.   He
thought, probably, that morning that he was a perfectly
honest man.   But when the Lord came and spoke to
him, he saw himself in an altogether different light.
Notice how short his speech was.   The only thing put
on record that he said, was this : " Behold, Lord, the half
of my goods I give to the poor; and if I have taken

anything from any man by false accusation, I restore him fourfold." A short speech ; but how the words have come ringing down through the ages !

By making that remark he confessed his sin—that he had been dishonest. Besides that, he showed that he knew the requirements of the law of Moses. If a man had taken what did not belong to him, he was not only to return it, but to multiply it by four. I think that men in this dispensation ought to be fully as honest as men under the Law. I am getting so tired and sick of your mere sentimentalism, that does not straighten out a man's life. We may sing our hymns and psalms, and offer prayers ; but they will be an abomination to God, unless we are willing to be thoroughly straightforward in our daily life. Nothing will give Christianity such a hold upon the world as to have God's believing people begin to act in this way. Zaccheus had probably more influence in Jericho after he made restitution, than any other man in it.

Finney, in his lectures to professing Christians, says : " One reason for the requirement, ' Be not conformed to this world,' is the immense, salutary, and instantaneous influence it would have, if everybody would do business on the principles of the Gospel. Turn the tables over, and let Christians do business one year on Gospel principles. It would shake the world ! It would ring louder than thunder. Let the ungodly see professing Christians in every bargain consulting the good of the person they are trading with—seeking not their own wealth, but every man another's wealth—living above the world—setting no value on the world any further than it would be the means of glorifying God : what do

you think would be the effect? It would cover the
world with confusion of face, and overwhelm them
with conviction of sin."

Finney makes one mark of genuine repentance
to be restitution. " The thief has not repented who
keeps the money he stole. He may have conviction, but
no repentance. If he had repentance, he would go and
give back the money. If you have cheated any one, and
do not restore what you have taken unjustly ; or if you
have injured any one, and do not set about to undo the
wrong you have done, as far as in you lies, you have not
truly repented."

In Exodus we read—" If a man steal an ox, or a
sheep, and kill it, or sell it, he shall restore five oxen
for an ox, and four sheep for a sheep." And again : " If
a man shall cause a field or vineyard to be eaten, and
shall put in his beast, and shall feed in another man's
field : of the best of his own field, and of the best of his
own vineyard, shall he make restitution. If fire break
out, and catch in thorns, so that the stacks of corn, or
the standing corn, or the field, be consumed therewith,
he that kindled the fire shall surely make restitution."

Or turn to Leviticus, where the law of the trespass-
offering is laid down—the same point is there insisted
on with equal clearness and force.

" If a soul sin, and commit a trespass against the Lord,
and lie unto his neighbour in that which was delivered
him to keep, or in fellowship, or in a thing taken away
by violence, or hath deceived his neighbour ; or have
found that which was lost, and lieth concerning it, and
sweareth falsely ; in any of all these that a man doeth,
sinning therein : then it shall be, because he hath sinned,

and is guilty, that he shall restore that which he took violently away, or the thing which he hath deceitfully gotten, or that which was delivered him to keep, or the lost thing which he found, or all that about which he hath sworn falsely ; he shall even restore it in the principal, and shall add the fifth part more thereto, and give it unto him to whom it appertaineth, in the day of his trespass offering."

The same thing is repeated in Numbers, where we read—" And the Lord spake unto Moses, saying, Speak unto the children of Israel, When a man or woman shall commit any sin that men commit, to do a trespass against the Lord, and that person be guilty ; then they shall confess their sin which they have done : and he shall recompense his trespass with the principal thereof, and add unto it the fifth part thereof, and give it unto him against whom he hath trespassed. But if the man have no kinsman to recompense the trespass unto, let the trespass be recompensed unto the Lord, even to the priest; beside the ram of the atonement, whereby an atonement shall be made for him."

These were the laws that God laid down for His people ; and I believe their principle is as binding to-day as it was then. If we have taken anything from any man, if we have in any way defrauded a man, let us not only confess it, but do all we can to make restitution. If we have misrepresented any one—if we have started some slander, or some false report about him—let us do all in our power to undo the wrong.

It is in reference to practical righteousness such as this, that God says in Isaiah—" Behold, ye fast for strife and debate, and to smite with the fist of wickedness : ye

shall not fast as ye do this day, to make your voice to be
heard on high. Is it such a fast that I have chosen ?—a
day for a man to afflict his soul? Is it to bow down his
head as a bulrush, and to spread sackcloth and ashes
under him ?—wilt thou call this a fast, and an acceptable
day to the Lord ? Is not this the fast that I have
chosen ?—to loose the bands of wickedness, to undo the
heavy burdens, and to let the oppressed go free, and that
ye break every yoke? Is it not to deal thy bread to the
hungry, and that thou bring the poor that are cast out to
thy house? when thou seest the naked, that thou cover
him ; and that thou hide not thyself from thine own
flesh ? Then shall thy light break forth as the morning, and thine health shall spring forth speedily : and
thy righteousness shall go before thee ; the glory of the
Lord shall be thy rereward. Then shalt thou call, and
the Lord shall answer ; thou shalt cry, and He shall say,
Here I am."

Trapp in his comment on Zaccheus, says, " Sultan
Selymus could tell his councillor Pyrrhus, who persuaded
him to bestow the great wealth he had taken from the
Persian merchants upon some notable hospital for relief
of the poor, that God hates robbery for burnt-offering.
The dying Turk commanded it rather to be restored to the
right owners ; which was done accordingly, to the great
shame of many Christians, who mind nothing less than
restitution. When Henry III. of England had sent the
Friar Minors a load of frieze to clothe them, they
returned the same with this message, 'that he ought not
to give alms of what he had rent from the poor; neither
would they accept of that abominable gift.' Master
Latimer saith, 'If ye make no restitution of goods

detained, ye shall cough in hell, and the devils shall laugh at you.' Henry VII. in his last will and testament, after the disposition of his soul and body, devised and willed restitution should be made of all such moneys as had unjustly been levied by his officers. Queen Mary restored again all ecclesiastical livings assumed to the crown, saying that she set more by the salvation of her own soul, than she did by ten kingdoms. A bull came also from the Pope, at the same time, that others should do the like ; but none did. Latimer tells us that the first day he preached about restitution, one came and gave him £20 to restore ; the next day another brought him £30 ; another time another gave him £200.

"Mr. Bradford, hearing Latimer on that subject, was struck in the heart for one dash of the pen which he had made without the knowledge of his master, and could never be quiet till, by the advice of Mr. Latimer, restitution was made, for which he did willingly forego all the private and certain patrimony which he had on earth. 'I, myself,' saith Mr. Barroughs, 'knew one man that had wronged another but of five shillings, and fifty years after could not be quiet till he had restored it.' "

If there is true repentance it will bring forth fruit. If we have done wrong to some one, we should never ask God to forgive us until we are willing to make restitution. If I have done any man a great injustice and can make it good, I need not ask God to forgive me until I am willing to do so. Suppose I have taken something that does not belong to me. I cannot expect forgiveness until I make restitution. I remember preaching in an American city, and a fine-looking man came up to me at the close. He was in great distress of mind. " The fact is," he said, " I am a defaulter. I have taken money that belonged to my employers. How can I become a Christian without restoring it?" " Have you got the money?" He told me had not got it all. He had taken about 1500 dollars, and he still had about 900. He said, " Could I not take that money and go into business, and make enough to pay them back?" I told him that was a delusion of Satan ; that he could not expect to prosper on stolen money ; that he should restore all he had, and go and ask his employers to have mercy upon him, and forgive him. " But they will put me in prison," he said. "Can you not give me any help?" " No ; you must restore the money before you can expect to get any help from God." " It is pretty hard," he said. " Yes, it is hard ; but the great mistake was in doing the wrong at first." His burden became so heavy that it was, in fact, unbearable. He handed me the money—950 dollars and some cents—and asked me to take it back to his employers. I told them the story, and said that he wanted mercy from them, not justice. The tears trickled down the cheeks of these two men, and they said, " Forgive him! Yes, we will be glad to forgive him." I went downstairs and brought him up. After he had confessed his guilt and been forgiven, we all fell down on our knees and had a blessed prayer-meeting. God met us and blessed us there.

There was another friend of mine in America who had come to Christ and was trying to consecrate himself and his wealth to God. He had formerly had transactions with the Government, and had taken advantage of them. This thing came to memory, and his conscience troubled him. He had a terrible struggle ; his conscience kept rising up and smiting him. At last he drew a

cheque for 1500 dollars and sent it to the Treasury of
the Government.   He told me he received such a blessing after he had done it.   That is bringing forth fruits
meet for repentance.   I believe a great many men are
crying to God for light; and they are not getting it
because they are not honest.

A man came to one of our meetings, when this subject
was touched upon.   The memory of a dishonest transaction flashed into his mind.   He saw at once how it
was that his prayers were not answered, but "returned
into his own bosom," as the Scripture phrase puts it.
He left the meeting, took the train, and went to a distant
city, where he had defrauded his employer years before.
He went straight to this man, confessed the wrong, and
offered to make restitution.   Then he remembered
another transaction, in which he had failed to meet the
just demands upon him ; he at once made arrangements
to have a large amount repaid.   He came back to the
place where we were holding the meetings, and God
blessed him wonderfully in his own soul.   I have not
met a man for a long time that seemed to have received
such a blessing.

Some years ago, in the north of England, a woman
came to one of the meetings, and appeared to be very
anxious about her soul.   For some time she did not seem
to be able to get peace.   The truth was, she was covering
up one thing she was not willing to confess.   At last,
the burden was too great ; and she said to a worker :
"I never go down on my knees to pray, but a few
bottles of wine keep coming up before my mind."   It
appeared, that years before, when she was housekeeper,
she had taken some bottles of wine belonging to her

employer. The worker said : " Why do you not make restitution ? " The woman replied that the man was dead ; and besides, she did not know how much it was worth. " Are there any heirs living to whom you can make restitution ? " She said there was a son living at some distance; but she thought it would be a very humiliating thing, so she kept back for some time. At last she felt as if she must have a clear conscience at any cost ; so she took the train, and went to the place where the son of her employer resided. She took five pounds with her ; she did not know exactly what the wine was worth, but that would cover it at any rate. The man said he did not want the money ; but she replied, " I do not want it : it has burnt my pocket long enough." So he agreed to take the half of it, and give it to some charitable object. Then she came back : and I think she was one of the happiest mortals I have ever met with. She said she could not tell whether she was in the body or out of it—such a blessing had come to her soul.

It may be that there is something in our lives that needs straightening out, something that happened perhaps twenty years ago, and that you had forgotten till the Spirit of God brought it to your remembrance. If you are not willing to make restitution, you cannot expect God to give you great blessing. Perhaps that is the reason why so many of your prayers are not answered.

" WHO would be cleansed from every sin,
    Must to God's holy altar bring
        The whole of life—its joys, its tears,
        Its hopes, its loves, its powers, its years,
    The will, and every cherished thing !

" Must make this sweeping sacrifice—
        Choose God, and dare reproach and shame.
        And boldly stand in storm or flame
    For Him who paid redemption's price ·
    Then trust (not struggle to believe),
        And trusting wait, nor doubt, but pray
        That in His own good time He'll say,
    ' Thy faith hath saved thee ; now receive.'

" His time is when the soul brings all,
        Is all upon His altar lain ;
        When pride and self-conceit are slain,
    And crucified with Christ, we fall
    Helpless upon His word, and lie ;
        When, faithful to His word, we feel
        The cleansing touch, the Spirit's seal,
    And know that He does sanctify."

                                    A. T. Allis.

CHAPTER V.

THANKSGIVING.

HE next thing I would mention as an element of prayer is THANKSGIVING. We ought to be more thankful for what we get from God. Perhaps some of you mothers have a child in your family who is constantly complaining—never thankful. You know that there is not much pleasure in doing anything for a child like that. If you meet with a beggar who is always grumbling, and never seems to be thankful for what you give, you very soon shut the door in his face altogether. Ingratitude is about the hardest thing we have to meet with. The great English poet says—

> " Blow, blow, thou winter wind,—
>   Thou art not so unkind
>   As man's ingratitude ;
>   Thy tooth is not so keen,
>   Because thou art not seen,
>   Although thy breath be rude."

We cannot speak too hardly of this evil, which so demeans those who are guilty of it. Even in Christians there is but too much of it to be seen. Here we are, getting blessings from God day after day : yet how little praise and thanksgiving there is in the Church of God !

Gurnall, in his *Christian Armour*, referring to the words "In everything give thanks," says : "' Praise is comely for the upright.' 'An unthankful saint' carries a contradiction with it. Evil and Unthankful are twins that live and die together ; as any one ceaseth to be evil, he begins to be thankful. It is that which God expects at your hands ; He made you for this end. When the vote passed in heaven for your being—yea, happy being in Christ !—it was upon this account, that you should be a name and a praise to Him on earth in time, and in heaven to eternity. Should God miss this, He would fail of one main part of His design. What prompts Him to bestow every mercy, but to afford you matter to compose a song for His praise ? 'They are My people, children that will not lie ; so He was their Saviour.'

"He looks for fair dealing at your hands. Whom may a father trust with his reputation, if not his child ? Where can a prince expect honour, if not among his favourites ? Your state is such that the least mercy you have is more than all the world besides. Thou, Christian, and thy few brethren, divide heaven and earth among you ! What hath God that He withholds from you ? Sun, moon, and stars, are set up to give you light ; sea and land have their treasures for your use ; others are encroachers upon them ; you are the rightful heirs to them ; they groan that any others should be served by them. The angels, bad and good, minister unto you ; the evil against their will, are forced like scullions when they tempt you, to scour and brighten your graces, and make way for your greater comforts; the good angels are servants to your heavenly Father, and disdain not to carry you in their arms. Your God withholds not Himself from you; He is your portion—Father, Husband, Friend. God is His own happiness, and admits you to enjoy Him. Oh, what honour is this for the subject to drink in his prince's cup! 'Thou shalt make them drink of the river of Thy pleasures.' And all this is not the purchase of your sweat and blood : the feast is paid for by Another, only He expects your thanks to the Founder. No sin-offering is imposed under the Gospel; thank-offerings are all He looks for."

Charnock in discoursing on Spiritual Worship, says : " The praise of God is the choicest sacrifice and worship, under a dispensation of redeeming grace. This is the prime and eternal part of worship under the Gospel. The Psalmist, speaking of the Gospel times, spurs on to this kind of worship; 'Sing unto the Lord a new song ; let the children of Zion be joyful in their King; let the saints be joyful in glory; let them sing aloud upon their beds ; let the high praises of God be in their mouth.' He begins and ends both psalms with *Praise ye the Lord!* That cannot be a spiritual and evangelical worship that hath nothing of the praise of God in the heart. The consideration of God's adorable perfections discovered in the Gospel will make us come to Him with more seriousness, beg blessings of Him with more confidence, fly to Him with a winged faith and love, and more spiritually glorify Him in our attendances upon Him. "

There is a great deal more said in the Bible about

praise than prayer ; yet how few praise-meetings there are! David in his Psalms always mixes praise with prayer. Solomon prevailed much with God in prayer at the dedication of the temple ; but it was the voice of *praise* which brought down the glory that filled the house : for we read—" And it came to pass, when the priests were come out of the holy place : (for all the priests that were present were sanctified, and did not then wait by course: also the Levites which were the singers, all of them of Asaph, of Heman, of Jeduthun, with their sons, and their brethren, being arrayed in white linen, having cymbals, and psalteries, and harps, stood at the east end of the altar, and with them a hundred and twenty priests sounding with trumpets :) It came even to pass, as the trumpeters and singers were as one, to make one sound to be heard in praising and thanking the Lord; and when they lifted up their voice with the trumpets, and cymbals, and instruments of music, and praised the Lord, saying, 'For He is good; for His mercy endureth for ever': that then the house was filled with a cloud, even the house of the Lord ; so that the priests could not stand to minister by reason of the cloud : for the glory of the Lord had filled the house of God."

We read too of Jehoshaphat, that he gained the victory over the hosts of Ammon and Moab, through praise, which was excited by faith and thankfulness to God.

" And they rose early in the morning, and went forth into the wilderness of Tekoa : and as they went forth, Jehoshaphat stood and said, ' Hear me, O Judah, and ye inhabitants of Jerusalem ; Believe in the Lord your

God, so shall ye be established ; believe His prophets, so shall ye prosper ' ; and when he had consulted with the people, he appointed singers unto the Lord, and that should praise the beauty of holiness, as they went out before the army, and to say, ' Praise the Lord ; for His mercy endureth for ever.' And when they began to sing and to praise, the Lord set ambushments against the children of Ammon, Moab, and Mount Seir, which were come against Judah ; and they were smitten."

It is said that in a time of great despondency among the first settlers in New England, it was proposed in one of their public assemblies to proclaim a fast. An old farmer arose ; spoke of their provoking heaven with their complaints ; reviewed their measures ; showed that they had much to be thankful for ; and moved that instead of appointing a day of fasting, they should appoint a day of thanksgiving. This was done; and the custom has been continued ever since.

However great our difficulties, or deep even our sorrows, there is room for thankfulness. Thomas Adams has said, " Lay up in the ark of thy memory not only the pot of manna, the bread of life ; but even Aaron's rod, the very scourge of correction, wherewith thou hast been bettered. Blessed be the Lord, not only giving, but also taking away, saith Job. God that sees there is no walking upon roses to heaven, puts His children into the way of discipline ; and by the fire of correction eats out the rust of corruption. God sends trouble, then bids us call upon Him ; promiseth our deliverance ; and lastly, the all He requires of us is to glorify Him. ' Call upon Me in the day of trouble ; I will deliver thee, and thou shalt glorify Me.'" Like the nightingale, we can sing in the night, and say with John Newton,—

> " Since all that I meet shall work for my good,
>   The bitter is sweet, the medicine food ;
>   Though painful at present, 't will cease before long,
>   And then—oh, how pleasant !—the conqueror's song."

Among all the apostles none suffered so much as Paul; but none of them do we find so often giving thanks as he. Take his letter to the Philippians. Remember what he suffered at Philippi; how they laid many stripes upon him, and cast him into prison. Yet every chapter in that Epistle speaks of rejoicing and giving thanks. There is that well-known passage : " Be careful for nothing; but in everything, by prayer and supplication, with thanksgiving, let your requests be made known unto God." As some one has said, there are here three precious ideas : " careful for nothing; prayerful for everything; and thankful for anything." We always get more by being thankful for what God has done for us. Paul says again : " We give thanks to God the Father of our Lord Jesus Christ, praying always for you." So he was constantly giving thanks. Take up any one of his Epistles, and you will find them full of praise to God.

Even if nothing else called for thankfulness, it would always be an ample cause for it that Jesus Christ loved us, and gave Himself for us. A farmer was once found kneeling at a soldier's grave near Nashville. Some one came to him and said : " Why do you pay so much attention to this grave ? was your son buried here ? " " No," he said. " During the war my family were all sick, I knew not how to leave them. I was drafted. One of

my neighbours came over and said : ' I will go for you ;
I have no family.' He went off. He was wounded at
Chickamauga. He was carried to the hospital, and
there died. And, sir, I have come a great many miles,
that I might write over his grave these words, ' *He died
for me.*' "

This, the believer can always say of his blessed
Saviour, and in the fact may well rejoice. " By Him, therefore, let us offer the sacrifice of praise continually, that
is, the fruit of our lips, giving thanks to His name "

> " SPEAK, lips of mine !
> And tell abroad
> The praises of thy God.
> Speak, stammering tongue !
>   In gladdest tone,
>   Make His high praises known.
>
> " Speak, sea and earth !
>   Heaven's utmost star,
>   Speak from your realms afar !
> Take up the note,
>   And send it round
>   Creation's farthest bound.
>
> Speak, heaven of heavens !
>   Wherein our God
>   Has made His bright abode.
> Speak, angels, speak !
>   In songs proclaim
>   His everlasting name.
>
> " Speak, son of dust !
>   Thy flesh He took
>   And heaven for thee forsook.
> Speak, child of death !
>   Thy death He died,
>   Bless thou the Crucified."—*Dr. Bonar.*

CHAPTER VI.

FORGIVENESS.

HE next thing is perhaps the most difficult of all to deal with—FORGIVENESS. I believe this is keeping more people from having power with God than any other thing—they are not willing to cultivate the spirit of forgiveness. If we allow the root of bitterness to spring up in our hearts against some one, our prayer will not be answered. It may not be an easy thing to live in sweet fellowship with all those with whom we come in contact; but that is what the grace of God is given to us for.

The disciples' prayer is a test of sonship; if we can pray it all from the heart we have good reason to think that we have been born of God. No man can call God Father but by the Spirit. Though this prayer has been such a blessing to the world, I believe it has been a great snare: many stumble over it into perdition. They do not weigh its meaning, nor take its facts right into their hearts. I have no sympathy with the idea of universal sonship—that all men are the sons of God. The Bible teaches very plainly that we are adopted into the family of God. If all were sons God would not need to adopt any. We are all God's by creation; but when people teach that any man can say, " Our Father which art in heaven," whether he is born of God or not, I think that is contrary to Scripture. "As many as are led by the Spirit of God, they are the sons of God." Sonship in the family is the privilege of the believer. " In this the children of God are manifest, and the children of the devil," says the Apostle. If we are doing the will of God, that is a very good sign that we are born of God. If we have no desire to do that will, how can we call God " Our Father "?

Another thing. We cannot really pray for God's Kingdom to come until we are in it. If we should pray for the coming of God's kingdom while we are rebelling against Him, we are only seeking for our own condemnation. No unrenewed man really wants God's will to be done on the earth. You might write over the door of every unsaved man's house, and over his place of business, " God's will is not done here."

If the nations were really to put up this prayer, all their armies could be discharged. They tell us there are some twelve millions of men in the standing armies of Europe alone. But men do not want God's will done on earth as it is in heaven; that is the trouble.

Now let me come to the part I want to dwell upon: " Forgive us our trespasses, as we forgive them that trespass against us." This is the only part of the prayer that Christ explained.

" For if ye forgive men their trespasses, your heavenly Father will also forgive you : But if ye forgive not men their trespasses, neither will your Father forgive your trespasses."

Notice that when you go into the door of God's kingdom, you go in through the door of forgiveness. I never knew of a man getting a blessing in his own soul, if he was not willing to forgive others. If we are unwilling to forgive others, God cannot forgive us. I do not know how language could be more plain than it is in these words of our Lord. I firmly believe a great many prayers are not answered because we are not willing to forgive some one. Let your mind go back over the past, and through the circle of your acquaintance: are there any against whom you are cherishing hard feelings? Is there any root of bitterness springing up against some one who has perhaps injured you? It may be that for months or years you have been nursing this unforgiving spirit: how can *you* ask God to forgive you? If I am not willing to forgive those who may have committed some single offence against me, what a mean, contemptible thing it would be for me to ask God to forgive the ten thousand sins of which I have been guilty!

But Christ goes still further. He says: "If thou bring thy gift to the altar, and there rememberest that thy brother hath aught against thee; leave there thy gift before the altar, and go thy way; first be reconciled to thy brother, and then come and offer thy gift." It may be that you are saying: "I do not know that I have anything against any one." Has any one anything against you? Is there some one who thinks you have done them wrong? Perhaps you have not; but it may be they think you have. I will tell you what I would do before I go to sleep to-night: I would go and see them, and have the question settled. You will find that you will be greatly blessed in the very act. Supposing you are in the right and they are in the wrong; you may win your brother or sister. May God root out of all our hearts to-day this unforgiving spirit!

A gentleman came to me some time ago, and wanted me to talk to his wife about her soul. That woman seemed as anxious as any person I ever met, and I thought it would not take long to lead her into the light; but it seemed that the longer I talked with her the more her darkness increased. I went to see her again the next day, and found her in still greater darkness of soul. I thought there must be something in the way that I had not discovered, and I asked her to repeat with me this disciples' prayer. I thought if she could say this prayer from the heart the Lord would meet her in peace. I began to repeat it sentence after sentence, and she repeated it after me, until I came to this petition, " Forgive us our trespasses, as we forgive them that trespass against us ; " there she stopped. I repeated it the second time, and waited for her to say it after me ; she said she could not do it. "What is the trouble?" She replied, " There is one woman I never will forgive." " Oh," I said, " I have got at your difficulty ; it is no use my going on to pray, for your prayers will not go higher than my head. God says He will not forgive you unless you forgive others. If you do not forgive this woman, God will never forgive you. That is the decree of heaven." She said, " Do you mean to say that I cannot be forgiven until I have forgiven her?" " No, I do not say it : the Lord says it ; and that is far better authority." Said she, "Then I will never be forgiven." I left the house without having made any impression on her. A few years after, I heard that this woman was in an asylum for the insane. I believe this spirit of unforgiveness drove her mad.

If there is some one who has aught against you, go at once and be reconciled. If you have aught against any one, write to them a letter telling them that you forgive them, and so have this thing off your conscience. I remember being in the inquiry-room some years ago; I was in one corner of the room talking to a young lady. There seemed to be something in the way; but I could not find out what it was. At last I said: "Is there not some one you do not forgive?" She looked up at me and said: "What made you ask that? Has any one told you about me?" "No," I said; "but I thought perhaps that might be the case, as you have not received forgiveness yourself." "Well," she said, pointing to another corner of the room, where there was a young lady sitting, "I have had trouble with that young lady; we have not spoken to each other for a long time." "Oh," I said, "it is all plain to me now; you cannot be forgiven until you are willing to forgive her." It was a great struggle. But then you know, the greater the cross the greater the blessing. It is human to err; but it is Christlike to forgive and to be forgiven. At last this young lady said: "I will go and forgive her." Strange to say, the same conflict had been going on in the mind of the lady in the other part of the room. They both came to their right mind about the same time. They met each other in the middle of the floor. The one tried to say that she forgave the other, but they could not finish; so they rushed into each other's arms. The four of us—the two seekers and the two workers—got down on our knees together, and we had a grand meeting. These two went away rejoicing.

Dear friends, is this the reason why our prayers are not answered? Is there some friend, some member of our family, some one in the church, we have not forgiven? We sometimes hear of members of the same church who have not spoken to each other for years. How can you expect God to forgive you?

I remember one town that Mr. Sankey and myself went into. For a week it seemed as if we were beating the air: there was no power in the meetings. At last I said one day that perhaps there was some one cultivating this unforgiving spirit. The Chairman of our Committee, who was sitting next to me, got up and left the meeting right in view of the audience. The arrow had hit the mark, and gone home to the heart of the chairman of the committee. He had had trouble with some one for about six months. He at once hunted up this man and asked him to forgive him. He came to me with tears in his eyes, and said: " I thank God you ever came here." That night the inquiry-room was thronged. The Chairman became one of the best workers I have ever known; and he has been active in Christian service ever since.

Several years ago the Church of England sent a devoted missionary to New Zealand. After a few years of toil and success, he was one Sabbath holding a communion service in a district where the converts had not long since been savages. As the missionary was conducting the service, he observed one of the men, jnst as he was about to kneel at the rail, suddenly start to his feet and hastily go to the opposite end of the church. By and by he returned, and calmly took his place. After service the clergyman took him on one side and asked the reason for his strange behaviour. He replied : " As I was about to kneel I recognized in the man next to me the chief of a neighbouring tribe, who had murdered my father, and drunk his blood ; and I had sworn by all the gods that I would slay that man at the first opportunity. The impulse to have my revenge, at the first, almost overpowered me; and I rushed away, as you saw me, to escape the power of it. As I stood at the other end of the room and considered the object of our meeting, I thought of Him who prayed for His own murderers : ' Father, forgive them ; for they know not what they do.' And I felt then I could forgive the murderer of my father, and came and knelt down at his side."

As one has said : " There is an ugly kind of forgive-ness in this world—a kind of hedgehog forgiveness, shot out like quills. Men take one who has offended, and set him down before the blow-pipe of their indigna-tion, and scorch him, and burn his fault into him ; and, when they have kneaded him sufficiently with their fists, then they forgive him."

The father of Frederick the Great, on his death-bed, was warned by M. Roloff, his spiritual adviser, that he was bound to forgive his enemies. He was quite troubled, and after a moment's pause said to the Queen : " You, Feekin, may write to your brother (the King of England) *after I am dead*, and tell him that I forgave him, and died at peace with him." " It would be better," M. Roloff mildly suggested, " that your majesty should write at once." "No," was the stern reply. "Write after I am dead. That will be safer."

Another story tells of a man who, supposing he was about to die, expressed his forgiveness to one who had injured him, but added : "Now you mind, if I get well, the old grudge holds good."

My friends, that is not forgiveness at all. I believe true forgiveness includes forgetting the offence—putting it entirely away out of our hearts and memories.

As Matthew Henry says : "We do not forgive our offending brother aright nor acceptably, if we do not forgive him from the heart; for it is that God looks at. No malice must be harboured there, nor ill-will to any ; no projects of revenge must be hatched there, nor desires of it, as there are in many who outwardly appear peaceable and reconciled. We must from the heart desire and seek the welfare of those that have offended us."

If God's forgiveness were like that often shown by us, it would not be worth much. Supposing God said : " I will forgive you, but I will never forget it ; all through eternity I will keep reminding you of it," we should not feel that to be forgiveness at all. Notice what God says : " I will remember their sin no more." In a passage in Ezekiel it is said that not one of our sins shall be mentioned : is not that like God ? I do like to preach this forgiveness—the sweet truth that sin is blotted out for time and eternity, and shall never once be mentioned against us. In another Scripture we read : " Their sins and iniquities will I remember no more." Then when you turn to the eleventh chapter of the Hebrews, and read God's roll of honour, you find that not one of the sins of any of those men of faith is mentioned. Abraham is spoken of as the man of faith ; but it is not told how he denied his wife down in Egypt: all that had been forgiven. Moses was kept out of the Promised Land because he lost patience ; but this is not mentioned in the New Testament, though his name appears in the Apostle's roll of honour. Samson, too, is named ; but his sins are not brought up again. Why, we even read of "righteous Lot :" he did not look much like a righteous man in the Old Testament story ; but he has been forgiven, and God has made him "righteous." If we are once forgiven by God, our sins will be remembered against us no more. This is God's eternal decree.

Brooks says of God's pardon granted to His people, "When God pardons sin, He takes it sheer away ; that if it should be sought for, yet it could not be found : as the prophet Jeremiah speaks : ' In those days, and in that time, saith the Lord, the iniquity of Israel shall be sought for, and there shall be none ; and the sins of Judah, and they shall not be found : for I will pardon them whom I reserve.' As David, when he saw in Mephibosheth the features of his friend Jonathan, took no notice of his lameness, or any other defect or deformity ; so God, beholding in His people the glorious image of His Son, winks at all their faults and deformities ; which made Luther say, ' Do with me what thou wilt, since Thou hast pardoned my sin.' And what is it to pardon sin, but not to mention sin ?"

We read in the Gospel of Matthew : "Moreover if thy brother shall trespass against thee, go and tell him his fault between thee and him alone : if he shall hear thee, thou hast gained thy brother." Then a little further on we read that Peter comes to Christ and says, " How oft

shall my brother sin against me, and I forgive him? till
seven times?" Jesus replied, "I say not unto thee, Until
seven times: but, Until seventy times seven." Peter did
not seem to think that *he* was in danger of falling into
sin; his question was, How often should I forgive my
brother? But very soon we hear that Peter has fallen.
I can imagine that when he did fall, the sweet thought
came to him of what the Master had said about forgiving
until seventy times seven. The voice of sin may be loud;
but the voice of forgiveness is louder.

Let us enter into David's experience, when he said:
"Blessed is he whose transgression is forgiven, whose
sin is covered. Blessed is the man unto whom the Lord
imputeth not iniquity, and in whose spirit there is no
guile. When I kept silence, my bones waxed old
through my roaring all the day long. For day and
night Thy hand was heavy upon me: my moisture is
turned into the drought of summer. I acknowledged
my sin unto Thee, and mine iniquity have I not hid. I
said, I will confess my transgressions unto the Lord;
and Thou forgavest the iniquity of my sin."

David could look below, above, behind, and before;
to the past, present, and future; and know that all was
well. Let us make up our mind that we will not rest
until this question of sin is for ever settled, so that we
can look up and claim God as our forgiving Father.
Let us be willing to forgive others, that we may be able
to claim forgiveness from God, remembering the words
of the Lord Jesus, how He said, "If ye forgive men their
trespasses, your heavenly Father will also forgive you:
but if ye forgive not men their trespasses, neither will
your Father forgive your trespasses."

"Now, oh joy ! my sins are pardoned !
    Now I can and do believe !
All I have, and am, and shall be,
    To my precious Lord I give ;
He aroused my deathly slumbers,
    He dispersed my soul's dark night ;
Whispered peace, and drew me to Him—
    Made Himself my chief delight.

" Let the babe forget its mother,
    Let the bridegroom slight his bride ;
True to Him, I'll love none other,
    Cleaving closely to His side.
Jesus, hear my soul's confession ;
    Weak am I, but strength is Thine ;
On Thine arms for strength and succour,
    Calmly may my soul recline ! "

                        Albert Midlane.

CHAPTER VII.

UNITY.

HE next thing we need to have, if we would get our prayers answered, is—UNITY. If we do not love one another we certainly shall not have much power with God in Prayer. One of the saddest things in the present day is the division in God's Church. You notice that when the power of God came upon the early Church, it was when they were all of one accord. I believe the blessing of Pentecost never would have been given but for that spirit of unity. If they had been divided and quarrelling among themselves, do you think the Holy Ghost would have come and those thousands been converted? I have noticed in our work, that if we have gone to a town where three churches were united in it, we have had greater blessing than if only one church was in sympathy. And if there have been twelve churches united, the blessing has multiplied fourfold : it has always been in proportion to the spirit of unity that has been manifested. Where there are bickerings and divisions, and where the spirit of unity is absent, there is very little blessing and praise.

Dr. Guthrie thus illustrates this fact ; he says, "Separate the atoms which make the hammer, and each would fall on the stone as a snowflake ; but welded into one, and wielded by the firm arm of the quarryman, it will break the massive rocks asunder. Divide the waters of Niagara into distinct and individual drops, and they would be no more than the falling rain ; but in their united body they would quench the fires of Vesuvius, and have some to spare for the volcanoes of other mountains."

History tells us that it was agreed upon by both armies of the Romans and the Albans to put the trial of all to the issue of a battle betwixt six brethren —three on the one side, the sons of Curatius, and three on the other, the sons of Horatius. While the Curatii were united, though all three sorely wounded, they killed two of the Horatii. The third began to take to his heels, though not hurt at all ; and when he saw them follow slowly, one after another, because of wounds and heavy armour, he fell upon them singly, and slew all three. It is the cunning sleight of the devil to divide us that he may destroy us.

We ought to endure much, and sacrifice much, rather than permit discord and division to prevail in our hearts. Martin Luther says, "When two goats meet upon a narrow bridge over deep water, how do they behave ? Neither of them can turn back again, neither can pass the other, because the bridge is too narrow ; if they should thrust one another they might both fall into the water and be drowned. Nature, then, has taught them that if the one lays himself down and permits the other to go over him, both remain unhurt. Even so people should rather endure to be trod upon than to fall into debate and discord one with another."

Cawdray says, "As in music, if the harmony of tones be not complete they are offensive to the cultivated ear; so if Christians disagree among themselves they are unacceptable to God."

There are diversities of gifts—that is clearly taught—but there is one Spirit. If we have all been redeemed with the same blood, we ought to see eye to eye in spiritual things. Paul writes:—"Now there are diversities of gifts, but the same Spirit. And there are differences of administrations, but the same Lord."

Where there is union I do not believe any power, earthly or infernal, can stand before the work. When the Church, the pulpit, and the pew, get united, and God's people are all of one mind, Christianity is like a red-hot ball rolling over the earth; and all the hosts of death and hell cannot stand before it. I believe that men will then come flocking into the Kingdom by hundreds and thousands. "By this," says Christ, "shall all men know that ye are My disciples, if ye have love one to another." If only we love one another, and pray for one another, there will be success. God will not disappoint us.

There can be no real separation or division in the true Church of Christ; they are redeemed by one price, and indwelt by one Spirit. If I belong to the family of God, I have been bought with the same blood, though I may not belong to the same sect or party as another. What we want to do is to get these miserable sectarian walls taken away. Our weakness has been in our division; and what we need is that there should be no

schism or division among those who love the Lord Jesus
Christ. In the First Epistle to the Corinthians we read
of the first symptoms of sectarianism coming into the
early Church :—

"Now I beseech you, brethren, by the name of our
Lord Jesus Christ, that ye all speak the same thing, and
that there be no divisions among you : but that ye be
perfectly joined together in the same mind and in the
same judgment. For it hath been declared unto me of
you, my brethren, by them which are of the house of
Chloe, that there are contentions among you. Now
this I say, that every one of you saith, I am of Paul ;
and I of Apollos ; and I of Cephas ; and I of Christ.
Is Christ divided ? was Paul crucified for you ? or were
ye baptized in the name of Paul ?"

Notice how one said, " I am of Paul ; " and another,
"I am of Apollos ; " and another, " I am of Cephas."
Apollos was a young orator, and the people had been
carried away by his eloquence. Some said Cephas, or
Peter, was of the regular Apostolic line, because he had
been with the Lord, and Paul had not. So they were
divided ; and Paul wrote this letter in order to settle the
question.

Jenkyn in his commentary on the Epistle of Jude
says : " The partakers of a ' common salvation,' who here
agree in one way to heaven, and who expect to be here-
after in one heaven, should be of one heart. It is the
Apostle's inference in Ephesians. What an amazing
misery is it, that they who agree in common faith should
disagree like common foes ! that Christians should live
as if faith had banished love ! This common faith should
allay and temper our spirits in all our differences. This

should moderate our minds, though there is inequality in earthly relations. What a powerful motive was that of Joseph's brethren to him to forgive their sin, they being both his brethren, and the servants of the God of his fathers! Though our own breath cannot blow out the taper of contention, oh, yet let the blood of Christ extinguish it!"

What a strange state of things Paul, Cephas, and Apollos, would find if they could come to the world to-day! The little tree that sprang up at Corinth has grown up into a tree like Nebuchadnezzar's, with many of the fowls of heaven gathered into it. Suppose Paul and Cephas were to come down to us now; they would hear at once about Churchmen and Dissenters. "A Dissenter!" says Paul, "what is that?" "We have got a Church of England; and then there are those who dissent from the Church." "Oh, indeed! are there two classes of Christians here, then?" "I am sorry to say there are a good many more divisions. The Dissenters themselves are split up. There are Wesleyans, Baptists, Presbyterians, and Independents, and so on; even these are all divided up." "Is it possible," says Paul, "that there are so many divisions?" "Yes; the Church of England is pretty well divided itself. There is the Broad Church, the High Church, the Low Church, and the High-Lows. Then there is the Lutheran Church; and away in Russia they have got the Greek Church, and so on." I declare I do not know what Paul and Cephas would think if they came back to the world; they would find a strange state of things. It is one of the most humiliating things in the present day to see how God's family is divided up. If we love the Lord Jesus

Christ the burden of our hearts will be that God may
bring us closer together, so that we may love one another
and rise above all party feeling.

In repairing a church in one of the Boston wards,
the inscription upon the wall behind the pulpit was
covered up. Upon the first Sabbath after repairs,
" little five-year old " whispered to her mother : " I know
why God told the paint-men to cover that pretty verse
up. It was because the people did not love another."
The inscription was : " A new commandment I give
unto you, that ye love one another."

A Boston minister says he once preached on " The
Recognition of Friends in the Future," and was told after
service by a hearer, that it would be more to the point
to preach about the recognition of friends here, as he had
been in the church twenty years and did not know any
of its members.

I was in a little town in America some time ago.
One night as I came out of the meeting, I saw another
building where the people were coming out. I said to a
friend, " Have you got two churches here ? "   " Oh yes."
" How do you get on ? "   " Oh, we get on very well."
" I am glad to hear that. Was your brother minister at
the meeting ? "   " Oh no ; we don't have anything to do
with each other. We find that is the best way." And
they called that " getting on very well." Oh, may God
make us of one heart and of one mind ! Let our hearts
be like drops of water flowing together. Unity among
the people of God is a sort of foretaste of heaven. There
we shall not find any Baptists, or Methodists, or Congre-
gationalists, or Episcopalians ; we shall all be one in
Christ. We leave all our party names behind us when

we leave this earth. Oh that the Spirit of God may speedily sweep away all these miserable walls that we have been building up !

Did you ever notice that the last prayer Jesus Christ made on earth, before they led Him away to Calvary, was that His disciples might all be one ? He could look down the stream of time, and see that divisions would come—how Satan would try to divide the flock of God. Nothing will silence infidels so quickly as Christians everywhere being united. Then our testimony will have weight with the ungodly and the careless. But when they see how Christians are divided, God will not work. The Holy Spirit is grieved, and there is little power where there is no unity.

If I thought I had one drop of sectarian blood in my veins, I would let it out before I went to bed ; if I had one sectarian hair in my head, I would pull it out. Let us get right to the heart of Jesus Christ ; then our prayers will be acceptable to God, and showers of blessings will descend.

> " LET party names no more be known
>   Among the ransomed throng ;
> For Jesus claims them for His own,
>   To Him they all belong.
>
> " One in their covenant Head and King,
>   They should be one in heart :
> Of one salvation all should sing,
>   Each claiming his own part.
>
> " One bread, one family, one rock,
>   One building, formed by love,
> One fold, one Shepherd, yea, one flock,
>   They shall be one above."
>
> *Joseph Irons.*

CHAPTER VIII.

FAITH.

NOTHER element is FAITH. It is as important for us to know how to pray as it is to know how to work. We are not told that Jesus ever taught His disciples how to preach, but He taught them how to pray. He wanted them to have power with God; then He knew they would have power with man. In James we read, "If any of you lack wisdom, let him ask of God . . . . and it shall be given him; but let him ask in faith, nothing wavering." So faith is the golden key that unlocks the treasures of heaven. It was the shield that David took when he met Goliath on the field; he believed that God was going to deliver the Philistine into his hands. Some one has said that faith could lead Christ about anywhere; wherever He found it He honoured it. Unbelief sees something in God's hand, and says, "I cannot get it;" Faith sees it, and says, "I will have it."

The new life begins with faith; then we have only to go on building on that foundation. "I say unto you, what things soever ye desire, when ye pray, believe that ye receive them, and ye shall have them." But bear in mind, we must be in earnest when we go to God.

I do not know of a more vivid illustration of the cry of distress for help going up to God, in all the earnestness of deeply realized need, than the following story supplies :—

Carl Steinman, who visited Mount Hecla, Iceland, just before the great eruption, in 1845, after a repose of eighty years, narrowly escaped death by venturing into the smoking crater against the earnest entreaty of his guide. On the brink of the yawning gulf he was prostrated by a convulsion of the summit, and held there by blocks of lava upon his feet. He graphically writes :

" Oh the horrors of that awful realization ! There, over the mouth of a black and heated abyss, I was held suspended, a helpless and conscious prisoner, to be hurled downward by the next great throe of trembling Nature !

" ' Help ! help ! help !—for the love of God, help ! ' I shrieked, in the very agony of my despair.

" I had nothing to rely upon but the mercy of heaven ; and I prayed to God as I had never prayed before, for the forgiveness of my sins, that they might not follow me to judgment.

" All at once, I heard a shout ; and, looking around, I beheld, with feelings that cannot be described, my faithful guide hastening down the sides of the crater to my relief.

" ' I warned you ! ' said he.

" ' You did ! ' cried I ; ' but forgive me, and save me ; for I am perishing !

" ' I will save you, or perish with you ! '

" The earth trembled, and the rocks parted—one of them rolling down the chasm with a dull, booming sound. I sprang forward ; I seized a hand of the guide ; and the next moment we had both fallen, locked in each other's arms, upon the solid earth above. I was free, but still upon the verge of the pit."

Bishop Hall, in a well-known extract, thus puts the point of earnestness in its relation to the prayer of faith :

" An arrow, if it be drawn up but a little way, goes not far ; but, if it be pulled up to the head, flies swiftly, and pierces deep. Thus prayer, if it be only dribbled forth from careless lips, falls at our feet. It is the strength of ejaculation and strong desire which sends it to heaven, and makes it pierce the clouds. It is not the arithmetic of our prayers, how many they are ; nor the rhetoric of our prayers, how eloquent they be ; nor the geometry of our prayers, how long they be ; nor the music of our prayers, how sweet our voice may be ; nor the logic of our prayers, how argumentative they may be ; nor the method of our prayers, how orderly they may be ; nor even the divinity of our prayers, how good the doctrine may be,—which God cares for. He looks not for the horny knees which James is said to have had through the assiduity of prayer. We might be like Bartholomew, who is said to have had a hundred prayers for the morning, and as many for the evening, and all might be of no avail. Fervency of spirit is that which availeth much."

Archbishop Leighton says : " It is not the gilded paper and good writing of a petition that prevails with a king, but the moving sense of it. And to that King who discerns the heart, heart-sense is the sense of all, and that which He only regards. He listens to hear what that speaks, and takes all as nothing where that is silent. All other excellence in prayer is but the outside and fashion of it. This is the life of it."

Brooks says: "As a painted fire is no fire, a dead man no man, so a cold prayer is no prayer. In a painted fire there is no heat, in a dead man there is no life; so in a cold prayer there is no omnipotency, no devotion, no blessing. Cold prayers are as arrows without heads, as swords without edges, as birds without wings; they pierce not, they cut not, they fly not up to heaven. Cold prayers do always freeze before they get to heaven. Oh that Christians would chide themselves out of their cold prayers, and chide themselves into a better and warmer frame of spirit, when they make their supplications to the Lord!"

Take the case of the Syrophenician woman. When she called to the Master, it seemed for a time as if He were deaf to her request. The disciples wanted her to be sent away. Although they were with Christ for three years, and sat at His feet, yet they did not know how full of grace His heart was. Think of Christ sending away a poor sinner that had come to Him for mercy! Can you conceive such a thing? Never once did it occur. This poor woman put herself in the place of her child. "Lord, help me!" she said. I think when we get so far as that in the earnest desire to have our friends blessed—when we put ourselves in their place—God will soon hear our prayer.

I remember, a number of years ago at a meeting, I

asked all those who wished to be prayed for to come
forward and kneel or take seats in front. Among those
who came was a woman. I thought by her looks that
she must be a Christian ; but she knelt down with the
others. I said : "You are a Christian, are you not ?"
She said she had been one for so many years. "Did
you understand the invitation ? I asked those only who
wanted to become Christians." I shall never forget the
look on her face as she replied, "I have got a son who
has gone far away ; I thought I would take his place to-
day, and see if God would not bless him." Thank God
for such a mother as that !

The Syrophenician woman did the same thing—
"Lord, help *me* !" It was a short prayer, but it went
right to the heart of the Son of God. He tried her
faith, however. He said : "It is not meet to take the
children's bread and cast it to dogs." She replied :
"Truth, Lord ; yet the dogs eat of the crumbs which
fall from their masters' table." "O woman, great is thy
faith !" What a eulogy He paid to her ! Her story will
never be forgotten as long as the Church is on the earth.
He honoured her faith, and gave her all she asked for.
Every one here can say, "Lord, help me !" We all need
help. As Christians, we need more grace, more love,
more purity of life, more righteousness. Are we not
hungering and thirsting after righteousness ? Then let
us make this prayer to-day. I want God to help me to
preach better and to live better, to be more like the Son
of God. The golden chains of faith link us right to the
throne of God, and the grace of heaven flows down into
our souls

I do not know but that woman was a great sinner ;

still the Lord heard her cry. It may be that up to this hour some of you have been living in sin ; but if you will cry, " Lord, help me ! " He will answer your prayer, if it is an honest one. Very often when we cry to God we do not really mean anything. You mothers understand that. Your children have two voices. When they ask you for anything you can soon tell if the cry is a make-believe one or not. If it is, you do not give any heed to it ; but if it is a real cry for help, how quickly you respond ! The cry of distress always brings relief. Your child is playing around, and it says, " Mamma, I want some bread ; " but it goes on playing. You know that it is not very hungry, so you let it alone. But, by and by, the child drops the toys, and comes tugging at your dress. " Mamma, I am so hungry." Then you know that the cry is a real one ; you soon go to the pantry, and get some bread. When we are in earnest for the bread of heaven, we will get it. This woman was terribly in earnest, therefore her petition was answered.

I remember hearing of a boy brought up in one of your almshouses. He had never learned to read or write, except that he could read the letters of the alphabet. One day a man of God came there and told the children that if they prayed to God in their trouble, He would send them help. After a time this boy was apprenticed to a farmer. One day he was sent out into the fields to look after some sheep. He was having rather a hard time, so he remembered what the preacher had said, and he thought he would pray to God about it. Some one going by the field heard a voice behind the hedge. They looked to see whose it was, and saw the little fellow on his knees, saying, " A, B, C, D," and so on. The man said, " My boy, what are you doing?" He looked up, and said he was praying. "Why, that is not praying; it is only saying the alphabet." He said he did not know just how to pray, but a man once came to the poor-house, who told them that if they called upon God He would help them. So he thought that if he named over the letters of the alphabet, God would take them and put them together into a prayer, and give him what he wanted. The little fellow was really praying. Sometimes, when your child talks, your friends cannot understand what he says; but the mother understands very well. So if our prayer comes right from the heart, God understands our language. It is a delusion of the devil to think we cannot pray; we can if we really want anything. It is not the most beautiful or the most eloquent language that brings down the answer: it is the cry that goes up from a burdened heart. When this poor Gentile woman cried out, " Lord, help me !" the cry flashed over the divine wires and the blessing came. So you can pray if you will; it is the desire, the wish of the heart, that God delights to hear and to answer.

Then we must *expect* to receive a blessing. When the centurion wanted Christ to heal his servant, he thought he was not worthy to go and ask the Lord himself, so he sent his friends to make the petition. He sent out messengers to meet the Master, and say, " Do not trouble yourself to come; all you have to do is to speak the word, and the disease will go." Jesus said to the Jews, " I have not found so great faith, no, not in Israel." He marvelled at the faith of this centurion ; it pleased Him, so that He healed the servant then and there. Faith brought the answer.

In John we read of a nobleman whose child was sick. The father fell on his knees before the Master, and said, "Come down, ere my child die." Here you have both earnestness and faith ; and the Lord answered the prayer at once. The nobleman's son began to amend that very hour. Christ honoured the man's faith.

In his case there was nothing to rest upon but the bare word of Christ ; but this was enough. It is well to bear always in mind, that the object of faith is not the creature, but the Creator ; not the instrument, but the hand that wields it.

Richard Sibbes puts it for us thus : "The object in believing is God, and Christ as Mediator. We must have both to found our faith upon. We cannot believe in God, except we believe in Christ. For God must be satisfied by God ; and by Him that is God must that satisfaction be applied—the Spirit of God—by working faith in the heart, and for raising it up when it is dejected. All is supernatural in faith. The things we believe are above nature ; the promises are above nature ; the worker of it, the Holy Ghost, is above nature ; and everything in faith is above nature. There must be a God in whom we believe, and a God through whom we may know that Christ is God—not only by that which Christ hath done, the miracles, which none could do but God, but also by what is done to Him. And two things are done to Him, which show that He is God— that is, faith and prayer. We must believe only in God, and pray only to God : but Christ is the object of both these. Here He is set forth as the object of faith, and of prayer in that of Saint Stephen : ' Lord Jesus, receive my spirit.' And, therefore, He is God ; for that is done unto Him which is proper and peculiar only to God. Oh, what a strong foundation, what bottom and basis our faith hath ! There is God the Father, Son, and Holy Ghost, and Christ the Mediator. That our faith may be supported, we have Him to believe on who supports heaven and earth."

" There is nothing that can lie in the way of the accomplishment of any of God's promises, but it is conquerable by faith."

As Samuel Rutherford says, commenting on the case of the Syrophenician woman : " See the sweet use of faith under a sad temptation ; faith trafficketh with Christ and heaven in the dark, upon plain trust and credit, without seeing any surety or pawn : ' Blessed are they that have not seen, and yet have believed.' And the reason is because faith is sinewed and boned with spiritual courage ; so as to keep a barred city against hell, yea, and to stand under impossibilities ; and here is a weak woman, though not as a woman, yet as a believer, standing out against Him who is ' the Mighty God, the Father of Ages, the Prince of Peace.' Faith only standeth out, and over- cometh the sword, the world, and all afflictions. This is our victory, whereby one man overcometh the great and vast world."

Bishop Ryle has said of Christ's intercession as the ground and sureness of our faith : " The bank-note with- out a signature at the bottom is nothing but a worthless piece of paper. The stroke of a pen confers on it all its value. The prayer of a poor child of Adam is a feeble thing in itself, but once endorsed by the hand of the Lord Jesus, it availeth much. There was an officer in the city of Rome who was appointed to have his doors always open, in order to receive any Roman citizen who applied to him for help. Just so the ear of the Lord Jesus is ever open to the cry of all who want mercy and grace. It is His office to help them. Their prayer is His delight. Reader, think of this. Is not this encouragement?

Let us close this chapter by referring to some of our Lord's own words concerning faith in its relation to prayer :

"And when He saw a fig-tree in the way, He came to it, and found nothing thereon, but leaves only, and said unto it, Let no fruit grow on thee henceforward for ever. And presently the fig-tree withered away. And when the disciples saw it, they marvelled, saying, How soon is the fig-tree withered away! Jesus answered and said unto them, Verily I say unto you, If ye have faith, and doubt not, ye shall not only do this which is done to the fig-tree, but also if ye shall say unto this mountain, Be thou removed, and be thou cast into the sea ; it shall be done. And all things whatsoever ye shall ask in prayer, believing, ye shall receive."

So again our Lord says : "Verily, verily, I say unto you, He that believeth on Me, the works that I do shall he do also ; and greater works than these shall he do ; because I go unto My Father. And whatsoever ye shall ask in My name, that will I do, that the Father may be glorified in the Son. If ye shall ask anything in My name, I will do it." And further : "If ye abide in Me, and My words abide in you, ye shall ask what ye will, and it shall be done unto you." "Verily, verily, I say unto you, whatsoever ye shall ask the Father in My name, He will give it you. Hitherto have ye asked nothing in My name ; ask, and ye shall receive, that your joy may be full."

"HAVE faith in God   for He who reigns on high
  Hath borne thy grief, and hears the suppliant's sigh:
  Still to His arms, thine only refuge, fly :
            Have faith in God !

" Fear not to call on Him, O soul distressed !
  Thy sorrow's whisper woos thee to His breast :
  He who is oftenest there is oftenest blest.
            Have faith in God !

" Lean not on Egypt's reeds : slake not thy thirst
  At earthly cisterns.   Seek the kingdom first.
  Though man and Satan fright thee with their worst,
            Have faith in God !

" Go, tell Him all ! The sigh thy bosom heaves
  Is heard in heaven.   Strength and peace He gives,
  Who gave Himself for thee.   Our Jesus lives:
            Have faith in God ! "
                              Anna Shipton.

CHAPTER IX,

PETITION.

THE next element in prayer that I notice is PETITION. How often we go to prayer-meetings without really asking for anything! Our prayers go all round the world, without anything definite being asked for. We do not expect anything. Many people would be greatly surprised if God did answer their prayers. I remember hearing of a very eloquent man who was leading a meeting in prayer. There was not a single definite petition in the whole. A poor earnest woman shouted out: "Ask Him summat, man." How often you hear what is called prayer without any asking! "Ask, and ye shall receive."

I believe if we put all the stumbling-blocks out of the way, God will answer our petitions. If we put away sin and come into His presence with pure hands, as He has commanded us to come, our prayers will have power with Him. In Luke's Gospel we have as a grand supplement to the "Disciples' Prayer": "Ask, and it shall be given you; seek, and ye shall find; knock, and it shall be opened unto you." . Some people think God does not like to be troubled with our constant coming and asking. The only way to trouble God is not to come at all. He encourages us to come to Him repeatedly, and press our claims.

I believe you will find three kinds of Christians in the Church to-day. The first are those who *ask* ; the second those who *seek* ; and the third those who *knock*.

"Teacher," said a bright, earnest-faced boy, "why is it that so many prayers are unanswered ? I do not understand. The Bible says, 'Ask, and ye shall receive ; seek, and ye shall find : knock, and it shall be opened unto you ;' but it seems to me a great many knock and are not admitted."

"Did you never sit by your cheerful parlour fire," said the teacher, "on some dark evening, and hear a loud knocking at the door? Going to answer the summons, have you not sometimes looked out into the darkness, seeing nothing, but hearing the pattering feet of some mischievous boy, who knocked but did not wish to enter, and therefore ran away ? Thus is it often with us. We ask for blessings, but do not really expect them ; we knock, but do not mean to enter ; we fear that Jesus will not hear us, will not fulfil His promises, will not admit us ; and so we go away."

"Ah, I see," said the earnest-faced boy, his eyes shining with the new light dawning in his soul : "Jesus cannot be expected to answer *runaway* knocks. He has never promised it. I mean to keep knocking, knocking, until He *cannot help opening the door.*"

"While the prayer of faith," said an eloquent Welsh preacher, "is sure to succeed, our prayers, alas ! too often resemble the mischievous tricks of children in a town, who knock at their neighbours' houses, and then run away. We often knock at mercy's door, and then run away, instead of waiting for an entrance and an answer. Thus we act as if we were afraid of having our prayers answered."

A great many people pray in that way; they do not wait for the answer. Our Lord teaches us here that we are not only to ask, but we are to wait for the answer; if it does not come, we must seek to find out the reason. I believe that we get a good many blessings just by asking; others we do not get, because there may be something in our life that needs to be brought to light. When Daniel began to pray in Babylon for the deliverance of his people, he sought to find out what the trouble was, and why God had turned away His face from them. So there may be something in our life that is keeping back the blessing; if there is, we want to find it out. Some one, speaking on this subject, has said, "We are to ask with a beggar's humility, to seek with a servant's carefulness, and to knock with the confidence of a friend."

How often people become discouraged, and say they do not know whether or not God does answer prayer! In the parable of the importunate widow, Christ teaches us how we are not only to pray and seek, but to find. If the unjust judge heard the petition of the poor woman who pushed her claims, how much more will our Heavenly Father hear our cry! A good many years ago an Irishman in the State of New Jersey was condemned to be hanged. Every possible influence was brought to bear upon the Governor to have the man reprieved; but he stood firm, and refused to alter the sentence.   One morning the wife of the condemned man, with her ten children, went to see the Governor.   When he came to his office, they all fell on their faces before him, and besought him to have mercy on the husband—the father. The Governor's heart was moved ; and he at once wrote out a reprieve.   The importunity of the wife and child saved the life of the man, just as the woman in the parable, who pressed her claims, induced the unjust judge to grant her request.

It was this that brought the answer to the prayer of blind Bartimeus.   The people, and even the disciples, tried to hush him into silence ; but he only cried out the louder, "Thou Son of David, have mercy on me ! " You notice that prayer is hardly ever mentioned in the Bible alone : it is prayer and earnestness ; prayer and watchfulness ; prayer and thanksgiving.   It is an instructive fact that throughout Scripture prayer is always linked with something else.   Bartimeus was in earnest ; and the Lord heard his cry.

Then the highest type of Christian is the one who has got clear beyond asking and seeking, and keeps knocking till the answer comes.   If we knock, God has promised to open the door and grant our request.   It may be years before the answer comes ; He may keep us knocking ; but He has promised that the answer will come.

I will tell you what I think it means to knock.   In an American city, a number of years ago, when we were having meetings, it came to a point where there seemed to be very little power.   We called together all the mothers, and asked them to meet and pray for their children.   About fifteen hundred mothers came together, and poured out their hearts to God in prayer. One mother said : " I wish you would pray for my two boys. They have gone off on a drunken spree ; and it seems as if my heart would break." She was a widowed mother. A few mothers gathered together, and said : " Let us have a prayer-meeting for these boys." They cried to God for these two wandering boys ; and now see how God answered their prayer.

That day these two brothers had planned to meet at the corner of the street where our meetings were being held. They were going to spend the night in debauchery and sin. About seven o'clock the first one came to the appointed place ; he saw the people going into the meeting. As it was a stormy night, he thought he would go in for a little while. The word of God reached him ; and he went into the inquiry-room, where he gave his heart to the Saviour.

The other brother waited at the corner until the meeting broke up, expecting his brother to come ; he did not know that he had been in the meeting. There was a young men's meeting in the church near by, and this brother thought he would like to see what was going on ; so he followed the crowd into the meeting. He also was impressed with what he heard, and was the first one to go into the inquiry-room, where he found peace. While this was happening, the first one had gone home to cheer his mother's heart with the good news. He found her on her knees. She had been knocking at the mercy-seat. While she was doing so her boy came in and told her that her prayers had been answered ; his soul was saved. It was not long before the other brother came in and told his story—how he, too, had been blessed.

On the following Monday night, the first to get up at the young converts' meeting was one of these brothers, who told the story of their conversion. No sooner had he taken his seat, than the other jumped up and said : "All that my brother has told you is true, for I am his brother. The Lord has indeed met us and blessed us."

I heard of a wife in this country who had an unconverted husband. She resolved that she would pray every day for twelve months for his conversion. Every day at twelve o'clock she went to her room alone and cried to God. Her husband would not allow her to speak to him on the subject ; but she could speak to God on his behalf. It may be that some of you have got a friend who does not wish to be spoken with about his salvation ; you can do as this woman did—go and pray to God about it. The twelve months passed away, and there was no sign of his yielding. She resolved to pray for six months longer ; so every day she went alone and prayed for the conversion of her husband. The six months passed, and still there was no sign, no answer. The question arose in her mind : Could she give him up ? "No," she said ; "I will pray for him as long as God gives me breath." That very day, when he came home to dinner, instead of going into the dining-room he went upstairs. She waited, and waited, and waited ; but he did not come down to dinner. Finally she went to his room, and found him on his knees crying to God to have mercy upon him. God convicted him of sin ; he not only became a Christian, but the Word of God had free course, and was glorified in him. God used him mightily. That was God answering the prayers of this

Christian wife ; she knocked, and knocked, till the answer came.

I heard something the other day that cheered me greatly. Prayer had been made for a man for about forty years ; but there was no sign of any answer. It seemed as though he was going down to his grave one of the most self-righteous men on the face of the earth. Conviction came in one night. In the morning he sent for the members of his family, and said to his daughter : " I want you to pray for me. Pray that God would forgive my sins ; my whole life has been nothing but sin— sin." And all this conviction came, as I have said, in one night. What we want is to press our case right up to the throne of God. I have often known cases of men who came to our meetings, and although they could not hear a word that was said, it seemed as though some unseen power laid hold of them, so that they were convicted and converted then and there.

I remember at one place where we were in America, a wife came to the first meeting and asked me to talk with her husband. " He is not interested," she said ; " but I am in hopes he will become so." I talked with him, and I think I hardly ever spoke to a man that seemed to be so self-righteous. It looked as though I might as well have talked to an iron post ; he seemed to be so encased in self-righteousness. I said to his wife that he was not at all interested. She said, " I told you that ; but I am interested for him." All the thirty days we were there that wife never gave him up. I must confess she had ten times more faith for him than I had. I had spoken to him several times ; but I could see no ray of hope. The last night but two the man came to me and said, "Would you see me in another room?" I went aside with him, and asked him what was the trouble. He said, "I am the greatest sinner in the State of Vermont." "How is that?" I said. "Is there any particular sin you have been guilty of?" I must confess I thought he had committed some awful crime, which he was covering up, and that he now wanted to make confession. "My whole life," he said, "has been nothing but sin. God has shown it to me to-day." He asked the Lord to have mercy on him; and he went home rejoicing in the assurance of sins forgiven. There was a man convicted and converted in answer to prayer. So if you are anxious about the conversion of some relative, or some friend, make up your mind that you will give God no rest, day or night, till He grants your petition. He can reach them, wherever they are—at their places of business, in their homes, or anywhere—and bring them to His feet.

Dr. Austin Phelps, in his "Still Hours," says, "The prospect of gaining an object will always affect thus the expression of intense desire. The feeling which will become spontaneous with a Christian under the influence of such a trust, is this : ' I come to my devotions this morning on an errand of real life. This is no romance, and no farce. I do not come here to go through a form of words; I have no hopeless desires to express. I have an object to gain; I have an end to accomplish. This is a business in which I am about to engage. An astronomer does not turn his telescope to the skies with a more reasonable hope of penetrating those distant heavens, than I have of reaching the mind of God, by lifting up my heart at the throne of grace.

This is the privilege of my calling of God in Christ
Jesus. Even my faltering voice is now to be heard in
heaven; and it is to put forth a new power there, the
results of which only God can know, and only eternity
can develop. Therefore, O Lord, thy servant findeth
it in his heart to pray this prayer unto Thee!'"

Jeremy Taylor says, "Easiness of desire is a great
enemy to the success of a good man's prayer. It must
be an intent, zealous, busy, operative prayer; for, consider what a huge indecency it is that a man should
speak to God for a thing that he values not! Our
prayers upbraid our spirits when we beg tamely for
those things for which we ought to die, which are more
precious than imperial sceptres, richer than the spoils of
the sea, or the treasures of Indian hills."

Dr. Patton, in his work on "Remarkable Answers to
Prayer," says, "Jesus bids us seek. Imagine a mother
seeking a lost child. She looks through the house, and
along the streets, then searches the fields and woods, and
examines the river-banks. A wise neighbour meets her
and says: 'Seek on, look everywhere; search every
accessible place. You will not find, indeed; but then
seeking is a good thing. It puts the mind on the
stretch; it fixes the attention; it aids observation; it
makes the idea of the child very real. And then,
after a while, you will cease to want your child.' The
words of Christ are, 'Knock, and it shall be opened unto
you.' Imagine a man knocking at the door of a house,
long and loud. After he has done this for an hour, a
window opens; and the occupant of the house puts out
his head and says: 'That is right, my friend: I shall not
open the door; but keep on knocking—it is excellent

exercise, and you will be the healthier for it. Knock away till sundown ; and then come again, and knock all to-morrow. After some days thus spent you will attain to a state of mind in which you will no longer care to come in.' Is this what Jesus intended us to understand, when He said ?—'Ask, and ye shall receive; seek, and ye shall find ; knock, and it shall be opened unto you.' No doubt one would thus soon cease to ask, to seek, and to knock ; but would it not be from disgust ? "

Nothing is more pleasing to our Father in heaven than direct, importunate, and persevering prayer. Two Christian ladies, whose husbands were unconverted, feeling their great danger, agreed to spend one hour each day in united prayer for their salvation. This was continued for seven years, when they debated whether they should pray longer, so useless did their prayers appear. They decided to persevere till death ; and, if their husbands went to destruction, it should be laden with prayers. In renewed strength, they prayed three years longer ; when one of them was awakened in the night by her husband, who was in great distress for sin. As soon as the day dawned, she hastened, with joy, to tell her praying companion that God was about to answer their prayers. What was her surprise to meet her friend coming to her on the same errand ! Thus ten years of united and persevering prayer was crowned with the conversion of both husbands on the same day.

We cannot be too frequent in our requests; God will not weary of His children's prayers. Sir Walter Raleigh asked a favour of Queen Elizabeth, to which she replied, " Raleigh, when will you leave off

begging ? " " When your Majesty leaves off giving,'
he replied. So long must we continue praying.

Mr. George Müller, in a recent address given by him
in Calcutta, said that in 1844, five individuals were laid
on his heart, and he began to pray for them. Eighteen
months passed away before one of them was converted.
He prayed on for five years more, and another was converted. At the end of twelve years and a half, a third
was converted. And now for forty years he had been
praying for the other two, without missing one single
day on any account whatever ; but they were not yet
converted. He felt encouraged, however, to continue in
prayer ; and he was sure of receiving an answer in relation to the two who were still resisting the Spirit.

> " SWEET is the precious gift of Prayer,
>   To bow before a throne of grace ;
> To leave our every burden there,
>   And gain new strength to run our race ;
> To gird our heavenly armour on,
> Depending on the Lord alone.
>
> " And sweet the whisper of His love,
>   When conscience sinks beneath its load,
> That bids our guilty fears remove,
>   And points to Christ's atoning blood ;
> Oh, then 'tis sweet indeed to know
> God can be just and gracious too.
>
> " But oh, to see our Saviour's face !—
>   From sin and sorrow to be freed !
> To dwell in His Divine embrace—
>   This will be sweeter far indeed !
> The fairest form of earthly bliss
> Is less than nought, compared with this."

CHAPTER X.

SUBMISSION.

NOTHER essential element in prayer is SUB-
MISSION.   All true prayer must be offered in
full submission to God.   After we have made
our requests known to Him, our language
should be, "Thy will be done."   I would a thousand times
rather that God's will should be done than my own.   I
cannot see into the future as God can ; therefore, it is a
good deal better to let Him choose for me than to
choose for myself.   I know His mind about spiritual
things.   His will is that I should be sanctified ; so I
can with confidence pray to God for that, and expect
an answer to my prayers.   But when it comes to tem-
poral matters it is different ; what I ask for may not be
God's purpose concerning me.

As one has well put it, " Depend upon it, prayer does
not mean that I am to bring God down to my thoughts
and my purposes, and bend His government according to
my foolish, silly, and sometimes sinful notions.   Prayer
means that I am to be raised up into feeling, into union
and design with Him ; that I am to enter into His
counsel, and carry out His purpose fully.   I am afraid

sometimes we think of prayer as altogether of an opposite character, as if thereby we persuaded or influenced our Father in heaven to do whatever comes into our own minds, and whatever would accomplish our foolish, weak-sighted purposes. I am quite convinced of this, that God knows better what is best for me and for the world than I can possibly know ; and even though it were in my power to say, '*My* will be done,' I would rather say to Him, '*Thy* will be done.'"

It is reported of a woman, who, being sick, was asked whether she was willing to live or die, that she answered, "Which God pleases." "But," said one, "if God should refer it to you, which would you choose?" "Truly," replied she, "I would refer it to Him again." Thus that man obtains his will of God, whose will is subjected to God.

Mr. Spurgeon remarks on this subject, "The believing man resorts to God at all times that he may keep up his fellowship with the Divine mind. Prayer is not a soliloquy, but a dialogue ; not an introspection, but a looking towards the hills, whence cometh our help. There is a relief in unburdening the mind to a sympathetic friend, and faith feels this abundantly ; but there is more than this in prayer. When an obedient activity has gone to the full length of its line, and yet the needful thing is not reached, then the hand of God is trusted in to go beyond us, just as before it was relied upon to go with us. Faith has no desire to have its own will, when that will is not in accordance with the mind of God ; for such a desire would at bottom be the impulse of an unbelief which did not rely upon God's judgment as our best guide. Faith knows that God's will is the highest good, and that anything which is beneficial to us will be granted to our petitions."

History informs us that the Tuṣculani, a people of Italy, having offended the Romans, whose power was infinitely superior to theirs, Camillus, at the head of a considerable army, was on his march to subdue them. Conscious of their inability to cope with such an enemy, they took the following method to appease him : They declined all thoughts of resistance ; set open their gates ; and every man applied himself to his proper business, resolving to submit where they knew it was in vain to contend. Camillus, entering their city, was struck with the wisdom and candour of their conduct, and addressed himself to them in these words : "You only, of all people, have found out the true method of abating the Roman fury ; and your submission has proved your best defence. Upon these terms, we can no more find in our heart to injure you than upon other terms you could have found power to oppose us." The chief magistrate replied, "We have so sincerely repented of our former folly, that in confidence of that satisfaction to a generous enemy, we are not afraid to acknowledge our fault."

In view of the difficulty of bringing our hearts to this complete submission to the Divine will, we may well adopt Fénélon's prayer, "O God, take my heart : for I cannot give it ; and when Thou hast it, keep it : for I cannot keep it for Thee ; and save me in spite of myself."

Some of the best men the world has ever seen have made great mistakes on this point. Moses could pray for Israel, and could prevail with God ; but God did not answer his petition for himself. He asked that God would take him over Jordan, that he might see Lebanon; and after the forty years' wandering in the wilderness he desired to go into the Promised Land ; but the Lord did not grant his desire. Was that a sign that God did not love him? By no means. He was a man greatly beloved of God, like Daniel ; and yet God did not answer this prayer of his. Your child says, " I want this or that ;" but you do not grant the request, because you know that it would be the ruin of the child to give him everything he wants. Moses wished to enter the Promised Land ; but the Lord had something else in store for him. As some one has said, God kissed away his soul, and took him home to Himself. " God buried him,"—the greatest honour ever paid to mortal man.

Fifteen hundred years afterwards God answered the prayer of Moses ; He allowed him to go into the Promised Land and to get a glimpse of the coming glory. On the Mount of Transfiguration, with Elijah, the great prophet, and with Peter, James, and John, he heard the voice come from the throne of God, " This is My beloved Son : hear ye Him." That was better than to have gone over Jordan, as Joshua did, and to sojourn for thirty years in the land of Canaan. So when our prayers for earthly things are not answered, let us submit to the will of God, and know that it is all right.

When one inquired of a deaf and dumb boy why he thought he was born deaf and dumb, taking the chalk he wrote upon the board, " Even so, Father ; for so it seemed good in Thy sight."

John Brown, of Haddington, once said, " No doubt I have met with trials like others ; but yet so kind has God been to me, that I think if He were to give me as

many years as I have lived in the world, I would not
desire one single circumstance in my lot changed,
except that I wish there had been less sin. It might
be written on my coffin, ' Here lies one of the cares of
Providence, who early lost both father and mother, and
yet never wanted for the care of either.' "

Elijah was mighty in prayer ; he brought fire down
from heaven on his sacrifice, and his petitions brought
rain on the thirsty land. He stood fearlessly before
King Ahab in the power of prayer. Yet we find him
sitting under a juniper tree like a coward, asking God
that He would let him die. The Lord loved him too
well for that ; He was going to take him up to heaven in
a chariot of fire. So we must not allow the devil to take
advantage of us, and make us believe that God does
not love us because He does not grant all our petitions
in the time and way we would have Him do.

As Moses takes up more room in the Old Testament
than any other character, so it is with Paul in the New
Testament, except, perhaps, the Lord Himself. Yet
Paul did not know how to pray for himself. He
besought the Lord to take away "the thorn in the flesh."
His request was not granted ; but the Lord bestowed on
him a greater blessing. He gave him more grace. It
may be we have some trial—some thorn in the flesh. If
it is not God's will to take it away, let us ask Him to
give us more grace, in order to bear it. We find that
Paul gloried in his reverses and his infirmities, because
all the more the power of God rested upon him. It may
be there are some of us who feel as if everything is
against us. May God give us grace to take Paul's
platform and say, " All things work together for good

to them that love God." So when we pray to God we must be submissive, and say, "Thy will be done."

In the Gospel of John we read: "If ye" (that "if" is a mountain to begin with,) "If ye abide in Me, and My words abide in you, ye shall ask what ye will, and it shall be done unto you." The latter part is often quoted, but not the first. Why, there is very little abiding in Christ now-a-days! You go and visit Him once in a while; but that is all. If Christ is in my heart, of course I will not ask anything that is against His will. And how many of us have God's Word abiding in us? We must have a warrant for our prayers. If we have some great desire, we must search the Scriptures to find if it be right to ask it. There are many things we want that are not good for us; and many other things we desire to avoid are really our best blessings. A friend of mine was shaving one morning, and his little boy, not four years old, asked him for his razor, and said he wanted to whittle with it. When he found he could not get it, he began to cry as if his heart would break. I am afraid that there are a great many of us who are praying for razors. John Bunyan blessed God for that Bedford jail more than for anything else that happened to him in this life. We never pray for affliction; and yet it is often the best thing we could ask.

Dyer says, "Afflictions are blessings to us when we can bless God for afflictions. Suffering has kept many from sinning. God had one Son without sin; but He never had any without sorrow. Fiery trials make golden Christians; sanctified afflictions are spiritual promotions."

Rutherford beautifully writes, in reference to the

value of sanctified trial, and the wisdom of submitting in it to God's will: "Oh, what owe I to the file, to the hammer, to the furnace of my Lord Jesus, who hath now let me see how good the wheat of Christ is that goeth through His mill and His oven, to be made bread for His own table! Grace tried is better than grace; and it is more than grace: it is glory in its infancy. I now see that godliness is more than the outside, and this world's passments and their bushings. Who knoweth the truth of grace without a trial? Oh, how little getteth Christ of us, but that which He winneth (to speak so) with much toil and pains! And how soon would faith freeze without a cross! How many dumb crosses have been laid upon my back, that had never a tongue to speak the sweetness of Christ, as this hath! When Christ blesseth His own crosses with a tongue, they breathe out Christ's love, wisdom, kindness, and care for us. Why should I start at the plough of my Lord, that maketh deep furrows on my soul? I know that He is no idle husbandman; He purposeth a crop. Oh that this white, withered lea-ground were made fertile to bear a crop for Him, by whom it is so painfully drest, and that this fallow ground were broken up! Why was I (a fool!) grieved that He put His garland and His rose upon my head—the glory and honour of His faithful witnesses? I desire now to make no more pleas with Christ. Verily He hath not put me to a loss by what I suffer; He oweth me nothing; for in my bonds how sweet and comfortable have the thoughts of Him been to me, wherein I find a sufficient recompense of reward! How blind are my adversaries who sent me to a banqueting house, to a house of wine, to the lovely feasts of my lovely Lord Jesus, and not to a prison, or place of exile ! "

We may close our remarks on this subject by a reference to the words of the Prophet Jeremiah, in Lamentations, where he says : " The Lord is good unto them that wait for Him, to the soul that seeketh Him. It is good that a man should both hope and quietly wait for the salvation of the LORD. It is good for a man that he bear the yoke in his youth. He sitteth alone and keepeth silence ; because he hath borne it upon him. He putteth his mouth in the dust ; if so be there may be hope. He giveth his cheek to him that smiteth him ; he is filled full with reproach. For the Lord will not cast off for ever : but though He cause grief, yet will He have compassion according to the multitude of His mercies. For He doth not afflict willingly, nor grieve the children of men. . . . . Who is he that saith, and it cometh to pass, when the Lord commandeth it not ? Out of the mouth of the most High proceedeth not evil and good ? Wherefore doth a living man complain, a man for the punishment of his sins ? Let us search and try our ways, and turn again to the LORD. Let us lift up our heart with our hands unto God in the heavens."

> " HEAR me, my God ; and if my lip hath dared
>   To murmur 'neath Thy hand, oh, teach me now
> To feel each inmost thought before Thee bared,
>   And this rebellious will in faith to bow.
> Though I wept wildly o'er the ruined shrine,
>   Where earthly idols held Thy place alone,
> Now purify and make this temple Thine,
>   And teach me, Lord, to say, ' Thy will be done!

" The waters that had slaked my burning thirst,
   In the wild wilderness forgot to flow ;
The gourd, whose growth I had too fondly nursed,
   Soon ceased its fruit and foliage to bestow ;
The fountains all were dry, but Thou didst bring
   My fainting steps unto Thy path once more ;
Thy love hath led me to that heavenly spring,
   And gently bade me ' drink, and thirst no more.

" Beneath the shelter of the gourd I dwelt,
   And in its beauty dreamt not of decay ;
But soon it withered ; then I trembling knelt—
   I knew the voice that bade it fade away.
I watched the blossoms drooping at Thy word
   In early morning ; and at noon was gone
E'en the last promise of its buds ! O Lord,
   My heart refused to say, ' Thy will be done !'

" Ere the fierce fervour of the day was spent,
   Thou, who didst bid my earthly shelter fade,
Had o'er my fainting head in mercy sent
   A cloud more welcome than love's fleeting shade ;
I blessed the hand that smote, the hand that healed,
   For not in vain hath died the sinless One,
Who with His precious blood our pardon sealed,
   And taught me, Lord, to say, ' Thy will be done !'

" What can I bring to offer that is mine ?
   A youth of sorrow, and a life of sin.
What can I lay upon Thy hallowed shrine,
   One hope of pardon for the past to win ?
While thus a suppliant at Thy feet I bow,
   Still dare I lift to Thee my tearful eyes,
I plead the promise of Thy word, that Thou
   A broken, contrite heart wilt not despise.

" What shall I bring ? a bruised spirit, Lord,
   Worn with the contest, pining now for rest,
And yearning for Thy peace, as some poor bird,
   'Mid the wild tempest, seeks its mother's breast
My sacrifice, the Lamb who died for me ;
   I plead the merits of Thy sinless Son ;
I bring Thy promises; I trust in Thee :
   In love Thou smitest ; Lord, ' Thy will be done !' "

CHAPTER X.

ANSWERED PRAYERS.

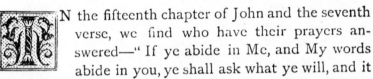N the fifteenth chapter of John and the seventh verse, we find who have their prayers answered—" If ye abide in Me, and My words abide in you, ye shall ask what ye will, and it shall be done unto you." Now in the fourth chapter of James, in the third verse, we find some spoken of whose prayers were not answered : " Ye ask, and receive not, because ye ask amiss." There are a great many prayers not answered because there is not the right motive ; we have not complied with the Word of God : we ask amiss. It is a good thing that our prayers are not answered when we ask amiss.

If our prayers are not answered, it may be that we have prayed without the right motive ; or that we have not prayed according to the Scriptures. So let us not be discouraged, or give up praying, although our prayers are not answered in the way we want them.

A man once went to George Müller and said he wanted him to pray for a certain thing. The man stated that he had asked God a great many times to grant him his request ; but He had not seen fit to do it. Mr. Müller took out his note-book, and showed the man the name of a person for whom, he said, he had prayed for twenty-four years. The prayer, Mr. Müller added, was not answered yet; but the Lord had given him assurance that that person was going to be converted, and his faith rested there.

We sometimes find that our prayers are answered right away while we are praying; at other times the answer is delayed. But especially when men pray for mercy, how quickly the answer comes! Look at Paul, when he cried, "O Lord, what wilt Thou have me to do?" The answer came at once. Then the Publican who went up to the Temple to pray—he got an immediate answer. The thief on the cross prayed, "Lord, remember me when Thou comest into Thy Kingdom!" and the answer came immediately—then and there. There are many cases of a similar kind in the Bible, but there are also others who prayed long and often. The Lord delights in hearing His children make their requests known unto Him—telling their troubles all out to Him : and then we should wait for His time. We do not know when that is.

There was a mother in Connecticut who had a son in the army; and it almost broke her heart when he left, because he was not a Christian. Day after day she lifted up her voice in prayer for her boy. She afterwards learned that he had been taken to the hospital, and there died; but she could not find out anything about how he had died. Years passed ; and one day a friend came to see some member of the family on business. There was a picture of the soldier boy upon the wall. He looked at it, and said, "Did you know that young man?" The mother said, "That young man was my son. He died in the late war." The man replied, "I knew him very well; he was in my company." The mother then asked, "Do you know anything about his end?" The man said, "I was in the hospital, and he died a most peaceful death, triumphant in the faith." The mother had given up hope of ever hearing of her lad; but before she went hence she had the satisfaction of knowing that her prayers had prevailed with God.

I think we shall find a great many of our prayers that we thought unanswered answered when we get to heaven. If it is the true prayer of faith, God will not disappoint us. Let us not doubt God. On one occasion, at a meeting where I was, a gentleman pointed out an individual and said, "Do you see that man over there? That is one of the leaders of an infidel club." I sat down beside him, when the infidel said, "I am not a Christian. You have been humbugging these people long enough; and making some of these old women believe that you get answers to prayer. Try it on me." I prayed; and when I got up, the infidel said with a good deal of sarcasm, "I am not converted; God has not answered your prayer!" I said, "But you may be converted yet." Some time afterwards I received a letter from a friend, stating that he had been converted and was at work in the meetings.

Jeremiah prayed, and said: "Ah, Lord God! behold Thou hast made the heaven and the earth by Thy great power and stretched-out arm, and there is nothing too hard for Thee." Nothing is too hard for God; that is a good thing to take for a motto. I believe this is a time of great blessing in the world; and we may expect great things. While the blessing is falling all around, let us arise and share in it. God has said, "Call unto Me, and I will answer thee, and show thee great and mighty things which thou knowest not." Now let us call on the Lord ; and let us pray that it may be done for Christ's sake—not our own.

At a Christian convention in America, a number of years ago, a leading man got up and spoke—his subject being "For Christ's Sake "—and he threw new light upon that passage. I had never seen it in that way before. When the war broke out the gentleman's only son had enlisted ; and he never saw a company of soldiers but his heart went right out after them. They started a Soldiers' Home in the city where that gentleman lived, and he gladly went on the committee, and acted as president. Some time afterwards he said to his wife, "I have given so much time to these soldiers that I have neglected my business ; " and he went down to his office with the fixed determination that he would not be disturbed by any soldier that day. The door opened soon after ; and he saw a soldier entering. He never minded him, but kept on writing ; and the poor fellow stood for some time. At last the soldier put down an old soiled piece of paper on which there was writing. The gentleman observed that it was the handwriting of his son and he seized the letter at once and read it. It was something to this effect : "Dear father, this young man belongs to my company. He has lost his health in defence of his country, and he is on his way home to his mother to die. Treat him kindly for Charlie's sake." The gentleman at once dropped his work and took the soldier to his house, where he was kindly cared for until

he was able to be sent home to his mother; then he
took him to the station, and sent him home with a
"God bless you, for Charlie's sake!"

Let our prayers, then, be for Christ's sake. If we
want our sons and daughters converted, let us pray that
it be done for Christ's sake. If that is the motive, our
prayer will be answered. If God gave up Christ for the
world, what will He not give us? If He gave Christ to
the murderers and blasphemers, and the rebellious of a
world lying in wickedness and sin, what would He not
give to those who go to Him for Christ's sake? Let
our prayer be that God may advance His work, not for
our glory—not for our sake—but for the sake of His
beloved Son whom He hath sent.

So let us remember that when we pray we ought to
expect an answer. Let us be looking for it. I remember
at the close of a meeting in one of our southern cities in
the United States, a man came up to me weeping and
trembling. I thought something I had said had aroused
him; and I began to question him as to what it was. I
found, however, that he could not tell a word of what I
had said. "My friend," said I, "what is the trouble?"
He put his hand into his pocket, and brought out a letter,
all soiled, as if his tears had fallen on it. "I got that
letter," he said, "from my sister last night. She tells me
that every night she goes down on her knees and prays
to God for me. I think I am the worst man in all the
Cumberland Army. I have been perfectly wretched
to-day." That sister was six hundred miles away; but
she had brought her brother to his knees in answer to
her earnest believing prayer. It was a hard case; but
God heard and answered the prayer of this godly sister,

so that the man was as clay in the hands of the potter. He was soon brought into the Kingdom of God—all through his sister's prayers.

I went off some thirty miles to another place, where I told this story. A young man, a lieutenant in the army, sprang to his feet and said, "That reminds me of the last letter I got from my mother. She told me that every night as the sun went down she prayed for me. She begged of me, when I got her letter, to go away alone, and yield myself to God. I put the letter in my pocket, thinking there would be plenty of time." He went on to say that the next news that came from home was that that mother was gone. He went out into the woods alone, and cried to his mother's God to have mercy upon him. As he stood in the meeting with his face shining, that lieutenant said: "My mother's prayers are answered: and my only regret is that she did not live to know it; but I will meet her by-and-by." So, though we may not live to see the answer to our prayers, if we cry mightily to God, the answer will come.

In Scotland, a good many years ago, there lived a man with his wife and three children—two girls and a boy. He was in the habit of getting drunk, and thus losing his situation. At last, he said he would take Johnnie, and go off to America, where he would be away from his old associates, and where he could commence life over again. He took the little fellow, seven years old, and went away. Soon after he arrived in America, he went into a public-house and got drunk. He got separated from his boy in the streets, and he has never been seen by his friends since. The little fellow was placed in an institution, and afterwards apprenticed in Massachusetts. After he had been there some time, he became discontented, and went off to sea; finally, he came to Chicago to work on the lakes. He had been a roving spirit, had gone over sea and land, and now he was in Chicago. When the vessel came into port, one time, he was invited to a Gospel meeting. The joyful sound of the Gospel reached him, and he became a Christian.

After he had been a Christian a little while, he became very anxious to find his mother. He wrote to different places in Scotland, but could not find out where she was. One day he read in the Psalms—" No good thing will He withhold from them that walk uprightly." He closed his Bible, got down on his knees, and said : " O God, I have been trying to walk uprightly for months past ; help me to find my mother." It came into his mind to write back to the place in Massachusetts, from which he had run away years before. It turned out that a letter from Scotland had been waiting for him there for seven years. He wrote at once to the place in Scotland, and found that his mother was still living ; the answer came back immediately. I would like you to have seen him when he got that letter. He brought it to me ; and the tears flowed so that he could scarcely read it. His sister had written on behalf of the mother ; she had been so overcome by the tidings of her long-lost boy that she could not write.

The sister said that all the nineteen years he had been away, his mother had prayed to God day and night that he might be saved, and that she might live to know what had become of him, and see him once more. Now, said the sister, she was so overjoyed, not only that he was alive, but that he had become a Christian. It was not long before the mother and sisters came out to Chicago to meet him.

I mention this incident to show how God answers prayer. This mother cried to God for nineteen long years. It must have seemed to her sometimes as though God did not mean to give her the desire of her heart; but she kept praying, and at last the answer came.

The following personal testimony was publicly given at one of our meetings lately held in London, and may serve to help and encourage readers of these pages.

"WITH GOD ALL THINGS ARE POSSIBLE."

A PRAYER-MEETING TESTIMONY.

I want you to understand, my friends, that what I state is not what I did, but what God did. *God only could have done it !* I had given it up, as a bad job, long before. But it is of God's great mercy that I am standing here to-night, to tell you that Christ is able to save *to the uttermost* all that come to God through Him.

The reading of those " Requests " [for the salvation of inebriates] touched me very deeply indeed. They seemed to be an echo of many a request for prayer which has been made for me. And, from my knowledge of society generally, and of human nature, I know that in a very great number of families there is need of some such request.

Therefore if what I may tell you will cheer any Christian heart, encourage any godly father and mother to go on praying for their sons, or assist any man or woman who has felt himself or herself beyond the reach of hope, I shall thank God for it.

I had very good opportunities. My parents loved the Lord Jesus, and did their best to train me up in the right path ; and for some time I thought myself that I should be a Christian. But I got away from Christ, and turned further and further away from God and all good influences.

It was at a public school where I first learned to drink. Many a time at seventeen I drank to excess; but I had an amount of self-respect that kept me from going thoroughly to the bad till I was about twenty-three : but from then till I was twenty-six, I went steadily down hill. At Cambridge I went on further and further in drinking, until I lost all self-respect, and voluntarily chose the worst of companions.

I strayed further and further from God, until my friends, those who were Christians and those who were not, considered, and told me that there was very little hope for me. I had been pleaded with by all sorts of people ; but I "hated reproof." I hated everything that savoured of religion, and I sneered at every bit of good advice or any kind word offered me in that way.

My father and mother both died without seeing me brought to the Lord. They prayed for me all the time they lived ; and, at the very last, my mother asked me if I would not follow her to be with her in heaven. To quiet and soothe her I said I would. But I did not mean it ; and I thought, when she had passed away, that she knew now my real feelings. After her death I went from bad to worse, and plunged deeper and deeper into vice. Drink got a stronger hold of me; and I went lower and lower down. I was never "in the gutter," in the acceptation in which that term is generally understood; but I was as low in my soul as any man who lives in one of the common lodging-houses.

I went from Cambridge first to a town in the north, where I was articled to a solicitor; and then to London. While I was in the north, Messrs. Moody and Sankey came to the town I lived in; and an aunt of mine, who was still praying for me after my mother's death, came and said to me, "I have a favour to ask of you." She had been very kind to me, and I knew what she wanted. She said, "It is to go and hear Messrs. Moody and Sankey." "Very good," I said; "it is a bargain. I will go and hear the men; but you are never to ask me again. You will promise that?" "Yes," she said, "I do." I went; and kept, as I thought most religiously my share of the bargain.

I waited until the sermon was over, and I saw Mr. Moody coming down from the pulpit. Earnest prayer had been offered for me; and there had been an understanding between my aunt and him that the sermon should apply to me, and that he would come and speak to me immediately afterwards. We met Mr. Moody in the aisle; and I thought that I had done a very clever thing when I walked round my aunt, before Mr. Moody could address me, and out of the building.

I wandered further from God after that; and I do not think that I bent my knees in prayer for between two and three years. I went to London; and things grew worse and worse. At times I tried to pull up. I made any number of resolutions. I promised myself and my friends not to touch the drink. I kept my resolutions for some days, and, on one occasion, for six months ; but the temptation came with stronger force than ever, and swept me further and further from the pathway of virtue. When in London I neglected my business and everything I ought to have done, and sank deeper into sin.

One of my boon-companions said to me, "If you don't pull up, you will kill yourself." "How is that?" I asked. "You are killing yourself ; for you can't drink so much as you used to." "Well," I replied, "I can't help it then." I got to such a state that I did not think there was any possible help for me.

The recital of these things pains me ; and as I relate them God forbid that I should feel anything but shame. I am telling you these things, because we have a Saviour ; and if the Lord Jesus Christ saved even me, He is able also to save you.

Affairs went on in this manner until, at last, I lost all control over myself.

I had been drinking and playing billiards one day ; and in the evening I returned to my lodgings. I thought that I would sit there awhile, and then go out again as usual. Before going out I began to think ; and the thought struck me—"How will all this end?" "Oh," I thought to myself, "what is the use of that? I know how it will end—in my eternal destruction—body and soul"!! I felt I was killing myself—my body ; and I knew, too well, what would be the result to my soul. I thought it impossible for me to be saved. But the thought came to me very strongly, "Is there any way of escape?" "No," I said ; "I have made any number of resolutions. I have done all I could to keep clear of drink; but I can't. It is impossible."

Just at that moment the words came into my mind, from God's own Word—words that I had not remembered since I was a boy: "With men this is impossible; but with God all things are possible." And then I saw, in a flash, that what I had just admitted, as I had done hundreds of times before, to be an impossibility, was the one thing that God had pledged Himself to do, if I would go to Him. All the difficulties came up in my way—my companions, my surroundings of all sorts, and my temptations; but I just looked up and thought, "It is possible with God."

I went down on my knees there and then, in my room, and began to ask God to do the impossible. As soon as I prayed to Him with very stammering utterance—I had not prayed for nearly three years—I thought, "Now then, God will help me." I took hold of His truth, I don't know how. It was nine days before I knew how, and before I had any assurance, or peace and rest, to my soul. I got up, there and then, with the hope that God would save me. I took it to be the truth, and I ultimately proved it; for which I praise God.

I thought the best thing I could do would be to go and get somebody to talk to me about my soul, and tell me how to be saved; for I was a perfect heathen, though I had been brought up so well. I went out and hunted about London; and it shows how little I knew of religious people and places of worship, that I could not find a Wesleyan chapel. My mother and father were Wesleyans, and I thought I would find a place belonging to their denomination; but I could not.

I searched an hour and a half; and that night I was in the most utter, abject, misery of body and soul any man can think of or conceive.

I came home to my lodgings and went upstairs, and thought to myself, " I will not go to bed till I am saved." But I was so ill from drinking—I had not had my usual amount of food in the evening; and the reaction was so tremendous, that I felt I must go to bed (although I dared not), or I should be in a very serious condition in the morning.

I knew how I should be in the morning, thinking, " What a fool I was last night!" when I would wake up moderately fresh, and go off to drink again, as I had often done. But again I thought, " God can do the impossible. He will do that which I cannot do myself." And I prayed to the Lord to let me wake up in much the same condition as that in which I went to bed, feeling the weight of my sins and my misery. Then I went to sleep. The first thing in the morning, as soon as I remembered where I was, I thought, " Has that conviction left me?" No; I was more miserable than before, and—it seemed strange, though it was natural—I got up, and thanked the Lord because He had kept me anxious about my soul.

Have you ever felt like that? Perhaps after some meeting or conversation with some Christian, or reading the Word of God, you have gone to your room miserable and " almost persuaded."

I went on for eight or nine days seeking the Lord. On the Saturday morning I had to go and tell the clerks. That was hard. I did it with the tears running down my cheeks. A man does not like to cry before other men. Anyway, I told them I wanted to become, and meant to become, a Christian. The Lord helped me with that promise, " With God all things are possible."

A sceptic dropped his head, and said nothing. Another fellow, with whom I played billiards, said, " I wish I had the pluck to say so myself ! " My words were received in a different way from what I thought they would be. But the very man who had told me that I was killing myself with drink, spent an hour and a half trying to get me to drink, saying, that I " had the blues, and was out of sorts ; and that a glass of brandy or whisky would do me good." He tried to get me to drink ; and I turned upon him at last, and said, " You remember what you said to me : I am trying to get away from drink, and not to touch it again." When I think of that I am reminded of the words of God Himself: "The tender mercies of the wicked are cruel."

And now the Lord drew me on until the little thread became a cable, by which my soul could swing. He drew me nearer ; until I found that He was my Saviour. Truly He is " able to save to the uttermost all that come unto God by Him."

I must not forget to tell you that I went down before God in my misery, my helplessness, and my sin, and owned to Him that it was impossible that I should be saved ; that it was impossible for me to keep clear of drink : but from that night to this moment, I have never had the slightest desire for drink.

It was a hard struggle indeed to give up smoking. But God, in His great wisdom, knew that I must have come to grief if I had to fight single-handed against the overwhelming desire I had for drink ; and He took that desire, too, clean away. From that day to this the Lord has kept me away from drink, and made me hate it most bitterly. I simply said that I had not any strength ; nor have I now : but it is the Lord Jesus who "is able also to save them to the uttermost that come unto God by Him."

If there is any one hearing me who has given up all hope come to the Saviour ! That is His name, for " He shall save His people from their sins." Wherever I have gone since then, I have found Him to be my Saviour. God forbid that I should glory ! It would be glorying in my shame. It is to my shame that I speak thus of myself ; but oh, the Saviour is able to save, and He will save !

Christian friends, continue to pray. You may go to heaven before your sons are brought home. My parents did : and my sisters prayed for me for years and years. But now I can help others on their way to Zion. Praise the Lord for all His mercy to me !

Remember, " with God all things are possible." And then you may say like St. Paul, "I can do all things through Christ which strengtheneth me."

> " O SOUL most desolate, look up ! For thee
> One faithful voice doth promise sure relief.
> Whate'er thy sin, whate'er thy sorrow be,
> Tell all to Jesus. He looketh where
> The weary-hearted weep, and draweth near
> To listen fondly to the half formed prayer,
> Or read the silent pleading of a tear.
> Lose not thy privilege, O silent soul ;
> Pour out thy sorrow at thy Saviour's feet.
> What outcast spurns the hand that gives the dole ?
> Oh, let Him hear thy voice ! to Him thy voice is sweet."
>
> *A. S.*